W9-CPP-358

04/24
STAND PRICE
$ 5.00

How to design a
Typeface

DESIGN MUSEUM

How to design a
Typeface

Previous page:
The Letter Plate Maker, a
sixteenth-century German
woodcut published by
Hartman Schopper.

How to design a Typeface

Introduction

Type is all around us. We encounter it every minute of the day, almost everywhere we look. It's on instrument panels and greetings cards, the sides of toasters and the sides of vans. It's on computer screens as our interface with the virtual world, and in our streets telling us where to go, what to do and when to do it.

As the design and arrangement of printed letterforms, typography is inextricably bound up with language. At the most basic level, that is because letters make up words and words are vehicles of communication. Yet change the way a word appears by altering the size, weight, spacing and style of the letters that comprise it, and different shades of meaning come into play.

UPPERCASE letters ask to be noticed. **Bold** letters are even more attention-seeking. *Italic* changes the emphasis. Fine print set in a small point size slips under the radar. Typefaces – serif, sans serif, slab serif, black letter, humanist, cursive – bring other layers of association and are the most potent element of all.

Right: Sebastian Lester (1972–) is a London-based type designer and typographic illustrator whose typefaces have been used by Intel, Dell, the *New York Times*, *The Sunday Times* and many other companies and publications worldwide. 'September', one of his limited-edition prints, was created by scanning in hundreds of drawings from his sketchbooks.

Overleaf: Our visual world is saturated with type. Typefaces are the means by which different messages compete for attention.

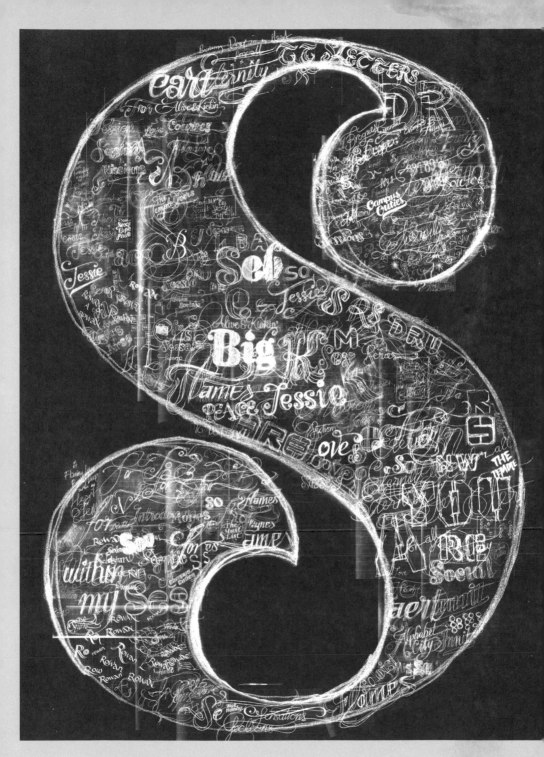

Principles

When Matthew Carter (1937–) designed Centennial for the Bell Telephone Company in 1974, he was trying to solve a particular problem of legibility in a densely printed text. His success can be gauged by the fact that the typeface is still in use. The 1999 poster by Stefan Sagmeister (1962–) for AIGA Detroit is a photograph of words that the designer slashed into his own skin. Both are usages of type. In between is a vast spectrum of different forms of communication.

Left: Matthew Carter's Bell Centennial was designed to replace Bell Gothic, the typeface previously used in Bell Telephone Company directories. These two sample settings show a comparison between the two. The new face is more legible and allows more entries to fit into a column. By condensing the address face in Bell Centennial, Carter has reduced the number of two-line entries by five in this example. Multiplied by the number of columns in the average directory, this space-saving measure represents a very considerable economy in paper consumption.

Right: Phone directories are printed at high speed on low-quality paper, which means that ink tends to spread, potentially affecting legibility. To compensate for this, Carter incorporated notches or 'ink traps' into the corners of letters.

6-POINT BELL GOTHIC

```
Vaught Donald L 542 39th St Short Wylam --780-8608
Vaught Ernest
  65 Merrimont Rd Hueytown --------491-6244
Vaught J C 625 Barclay Ln --------836-2436
Vaught Joe Jr Stertt --------672-2919
Vaught Ralph L 700 77th Wy S --------836-8452
Vaught Susan A 2109 46th Pl Central Pk ----787-4227
Vaultz Eva 1543 Dennison Av SW --------925-1752
Vause S F 603 Huckleberry Ln--------979-5289
Vause Stephen F 445 Shades Crest Rd----823-2662
Vautier Harold G 204 Killough Sprngs Rd ----853-5626
Vautrot Ruby L Mrs 2021 10th Av S -------933-2265
Vazquez Norberto
  Old Jasper Hwy Adamsvle --------674-3370
Veach J L 5725 Belmont Dr --------956-3990
Veach Loren Aldrich--------665-1831
Veal Ad 450 21st Av S --------251-9049
Veal Ad rlest 1711 Pinson --------841-7380
Veal B Evan atty 1711 Pinson --------841-2789
Veal Clarence E Garndle --------631-3856
VEAL CONVENTION SERVICES—
  1711 Pinson --------841-2789
  2109 10th Av N --------322-6102
Veazey W B Vincent --------672-9506
Veazey Wilbur E 1541 53rd St Ensley --------923-1960
Veazey William A 287--A Chastaine Cir----942-4137
Veazey Willie J 3084 Whispering Pines Cir --823-5795
Vebber Mark H 5216 Goldmar Dr --------956-1661
Vebco contr 1900 28th Av S Homewood ----879-2259
Vedel Dental Technicians Inc lab
  1116 5th Av N --------322-5475
Vedel George C 3848 Cromwell Dr --------967-2832
Vedel George C Jr 744 Saulter Ln --------871-8234
  Resf34744 Saulter Ln --------870-9758
Vedel Murrey B 612 Oakmoor Dr --------942-3619
Vedell Collen J Daisy City --------674-7772
Vedell William L 8830 Valley Hill Dr --------833-9915
Veenschoten & Co mfrs agts 2930 7th Av S -251-3567
Veenschoten L A 1919—D Tree Top Ln --------822-7109
Veenschoten W E 3240 Pine Ridge Rd ----871-8883
Vega Abraham 915 16th S --------933-7619
Vega Delores 2—B Watertown Cir----836-5980
Vega Edwin 2116 Rockland Dr Bluff Park --823-0403
Vegetable Patch Number 1 The
  Highway 31 S Alabstr --------663-7618
Vegetable Patch Office Alabstr --------663-7378
Vegetable Patch The Number 2 Dogwood --665-4179
Veigl Patrick B Pawnee --------841-1238
Veitch Beulah 1172 Five Mile Rd --------853-3361
Vest W L 4708 Lewisbrg Rd --------841-7402
Vest W T 4737 N 68th --------836-6371
Vesta Villa Exxon Self Serve
  1500 Hwy 31 S--------823-5008
VESTAVIA AMOCO SERVICE
  1456 Montgomery Hwy --------823-1213
VESTAVIA BARBEQUE & LOUNGE
  610 Montgomery Hwy Vestavia ------822-9984
Vestavia Barber Shop
  610--A Montgomery Hwy --------823-1974
VESTAVIA BEAUTY SALON
  710 Montgomery Hwy --------823-1893
Vestavia Beverage Co
  623 Montgomery Hwy --------822-9847
VESTAVIA BOWL
  Montgomery Hwy S Vestavia ------979-4420
Vestavia Church Of Christ
  2325 Columbiana Rd --------822-0018
VESTAVIA CHURCH OF GOD
  2575 Columbiana Rd --------823-1895
Vestavia Church Of God Day Care day
  nursry 2575 Columbiana Rd --------823-1895

VESTAVIA CITY OF---See Vestavia
  Hills City Of
```

BELL CENTENNIAL-1

```
Vaught Donald L 542 39th St Short Wylam --- 780-8605
Vaught Ernest 65 Merrimont Rd Hueytown --- 491-6244
Vaught J C 625 Barclay Ln -- 836-2436
Vaught Joe Jr Stertt -- 672-2919
Vaught Ralph L 700 77th Wy S -- 836-8452
Vaught Susan A 2109 46th Pl Central Pk -- 787-4227
Vaultz Eva 1543 Dennison Av SW -- 925-1752
Vause S F 603 Huckleberry Ln -- 979-5289
Vause Stephen F 445 Shades Crest Rd -- 823-2662
Vautier Harold G 204 Killough Sprngs Rd -- 853-5626
Vautrot Ruby L Mrs 2021 10th Av S -- 933-2265
Vasquez Norberto Old Jasper Hwy Adamsvle -- 674-3370
Veach J L 5725 Belmont Dr -- 956-3990
Veach Loren Aldrich -- 665-1831
Veal Ad 450 21st Av S -- 251-9049
Veal Ad rlest 1711 Pinson -- 841-7380
Veal B Evan atty 1711 Pinson -- 841-2789
Veal Clarence E Garndle -- 631-3856
VEAL CONVENTION SERVICES—
  1711 Pinson -- 841-2789
  2109 10th Av N -- 322-6102
Veazey W B Vincent -- 672-9506
Veazey Wilbur E 1541 53rd St Ensley -- 923-1960
Veazey William A 287—A Chastaine Cir -- 942-4137
Veazey Willie J 3084 Whispering Pines Cir -- 823-5795
Vebber Mark H 5216 Goldmar Dr -- 956-1661
Vebco contr 1900 28th Av S Homewood -- 879-2259
Vedel Dental Technicians Inc lab
  1116 5th Av N -- 322-5475
Vedel George C 3848 Cromwell Dr -- 967-2832
Vedel George C Jr 744 Saulter Ln -- 871-8234
  Resf34744 Saulter Ln -- 870-9758
Vedel Murrey B 612 Oakmoor Dr -- 942-3619
Vedell Collen J Daisy City -- 674-7772
Vedell William L 8830 Valley Hill Dr -- 833-9915
Veenschoten & Co mfrs agts 2930 7th Av S -- 251-3567
Veenschoten L A 1919—D Tree Top Ln -- 822-7109
Veenschoten W E 3240 Pine Ridge Rd -- 871-8883
Vega Abraham 915 16th S -- 933-7619
Vega Delores 2—B Watertown Cir -- 836-5980
Vega Edwin 2116 Rockland Dr Bluff Park -- 823-0403
Vegetable Patch Number 1 The
  Highway 31 S Alabstr -- 663-7618
Vegetable Patch Office Alabstr -- 663-7378
Vegetable Patch The Number 2 Dogwood -- 665-4179
Veigl Patrick B Pawnee -- 841-1238
Veitch Beulah 1172 Five Mile Rd -- 853-3361
Vest W L 4708 Lewisbrg Rd -- 841-7402
Vest W T 4737 N 68th -- 836-6371
Vesta Villa Exxon Self Serve 1500 Hwy 31 S -- 823-5008
VESTAVIA AMOCO SERVICE
  1456 Montgomery Hwy -- 823-1213
VESTAVIA BARBEQUE & LOUNGE
  610 Montgomery Hwy Vestavia -- 822-9984
Vestavia Barber Shop
  610--A Montgomery Hwy -- 823-1974
VESTAVIA BEAUTY SALON
  710 Montgomery Hwy -- 823-1893
Vestavia Beverage Co 623 Montgomery Hwy -- 822-9847
VESTAVIA BOWL
  Montgomery Hwy S Vestavia -- 979-4420
Vestavia Church Of Christ
  2325 Columbiana Rd -- 822-0018
VESTAVIA CHURCH OF GOD
  2575 Columbiana Rd -- 823-1895
Vestavia Church Of God Day Care day
  nursry 2575 Columbiana Rd -- 823-1895

VESTAVIA CITY OF---See Vestavia
  Hills City Of
VESTAVIA COIFFEURS
  617 Montgomery Hwy Vestva -- 823-1104
Vestavia Country Club--
  Shades Mountain -- 823-2451
```

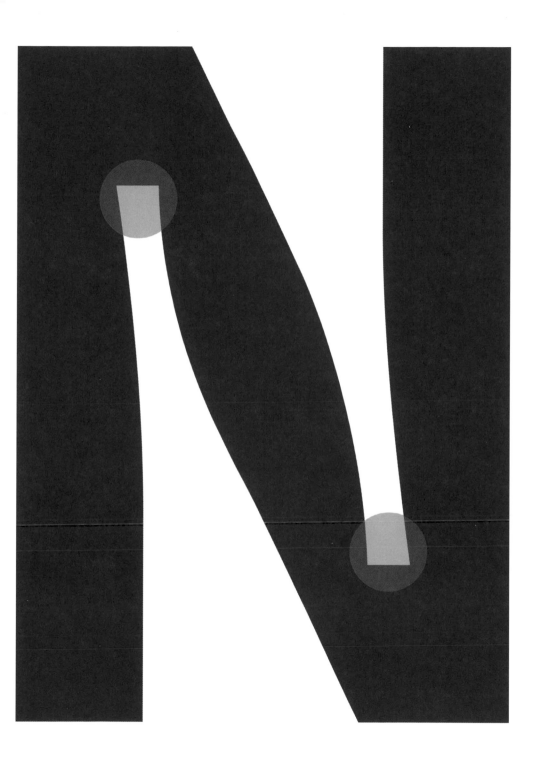

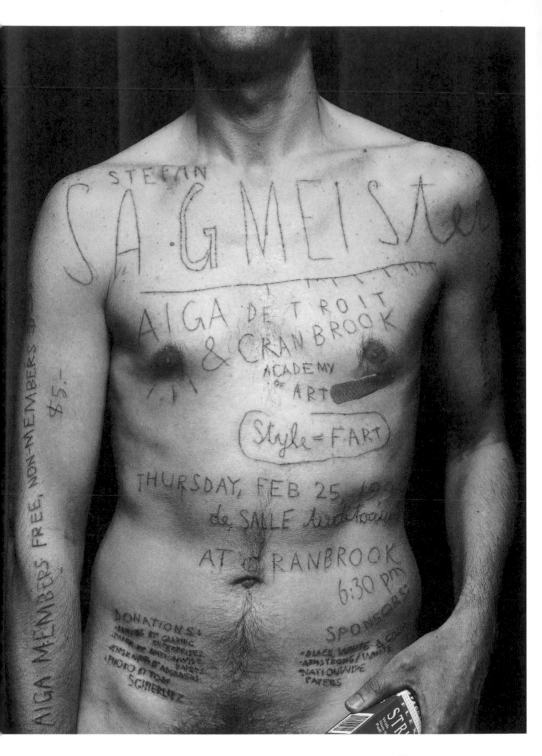

12

Left: Lecture poster for AIGA
Detroit (1999), art-directed
by Stefan Sagmeister and
photographed by Tom
Schierlitz. According to
Sagmeister, the idea behind
the image was to express
the pain that accompanied
most of their design projects.
The type was cut into
Sagmeister's skin by his
intern, Martin.

Right: Poster announcing
the release of *Set the Twilight
Reeling*, an album by
Lou Reed (1996), designed
and art-directed by
Stefan Sagmeister and
photographed by Timothy
Greenfield Sanders. Writing
the lyrics directly over
Lou Reed's face was a
way of conveying their
extremely personal nature.

THE TIMES

No. 46,254   LONDON MONDAY OCTOBER 3 1932   PRICE (Including) 4d

BIRTHS

MARRIAGES

DEATHS

SILVER WEDDING

DEATHS

DEATHS (continued)

IN MEMORIAM

ON ACTIVE SERVICE

PERSONAL

PERSONAL

PERSONAL

BUSINESS OFFERS

KENNEL FARM AND AVIARY

DOGS

CATS

FARM

MOTOR-CAR HIRE SERVICE

GARDENING, &c.

HOSPITAL NURSES

CLUB ANNOUNCEMENTS

CHEPSTOW RACE CLUB,

HELLENIC TRAVELLERS' CLUB

SOCIETIES

INVESTMENTS AND LOANS

BUSINESSES FOR SALE

DIRECTORS AND PARTNERS

ROAD TRANSPORT

WANTED

CLOTHES VALETING

CLASSIFIED ADVERTISEMENTS INDEX

Left: Times New Roman was
designed by Stanley Morison
in 1931–2 for *The Times*
newspaper. Legibility is a
particular concern where
type is set in small sizes and
arranged in columns. Until
the mid-1960s the front page
of the paper was devoted to
personal notices and small
advertisements.

Legibility

In the same way as researchers in the early decades of the
twentieth century studied people at work to determine the optimum
arrangement of the factory production line, and came up with
various ergonomic principles that would eventually be applied
to kitchen layouts and the design of desk chairs, scientists have
sought to understand which letterforms promote reading ease
and speed – in other words, what makes type legible.

Legibility matters. If you are driving down a motorway at 70mph, you
need to be able to read the road sign that says your exit is coming
up. If you are reading a report, a newspaper or a novel, or working
on screen, you don't want to have to work too hard to decode the
information you are trying to absorb. When Stanley Morison (1889–
1967) designed Times New Roman in 1931–2 for *The Times,* the
brief was to come up with a face that would be easy to read when
set in a small size and laid out in columns.

The style of the typeface, the size it is set in, its spacing and weight
all contribute to the legibility of text. So, too, can the *apparent* size
of a font, which is often a function of the 'x-height', or the size of a
lower-case 'x' from head to foot. Text set in lower case is
supposedly more legible than text set all in capitals. Roman type
is said to be more legible than italics. Contrast is also a factor.
Black on white is easier to read than reversed type. Poor setting
can also undermine the legibility of an otherwise clear typeface.

But can legibility be scientifically analysed? People who have a
visual impairment say that they find sans-serifs clearer and less
ambiguous. On the other hand, serifs are often cited as promoting
legibility – the little tails and flicks lead the eye comfortably from
one letter to another. Then there are those who point out that if a
typeface doesn't appeal to its target audience, it falls at the first
fence. All of which seems to indicate that in some circumstances
legibility is in the eye of the beholder.

Left: The typefaces employed on road signage need to be clearly legible at a distance and at speed.

Below left: The United States Federal Highway Administration developed the FHWA series of fonts in 1949 for use on highway signage. Often known as 'Highway Gothic', this set of sans-serif fonts was designed specifically for legibility. 'Interstate' (1993–4) by Tobias Frere-Jones (1970–) is a modern typeface based on Highway Gothic.

Below right: In 1968 the Swiss type designer Adrian Frutiger (1928–) was commissioned by Aeroports de Paris to design new signage for Charles de Gaulle International Airport. The result was Frutiger, completed in 1975 and now widely used around the world. In Britain, for example, Frutiger is the typeface of the National Health Service.

Context undoubtedly plays a part. A typeface on a CD cover that expresses a musical style and connects with the fans of a particular band or performer is doing a very different job from the typeface on a motorway sign or in a cookery book. Readers on screen are notably less patient than readers of print. In this context, research has shown that legibility has less to do with the clarity of screenfonts and more to do with expectations. Reading on screen, where users jump from link to link, is more like searching than turning a page. On screen, legibility might be seen as a function of how well type and layout promote that form of activity.

Custom also has a bearing on what we find legible. While familiar faces are easier to read, that same familiarity can breed contempt. When legibility becomes monotonous, a typeface can say '*Don't* read me'.

YOUNG KNIVES TRY EVERYTHING ONCE EXCEPT FOLK DANCING AND INCEST

ABCDEFGHIJKLMNOPQRSTUVWXYZ
ABCDEFGHIJKLMNOPQRSTUVWXYZ

For British band Young Knives' Mercury-nominated debut album, *Voices of Animals and Men*, the graphic design duo Tappin Gofton created a bespoke typeface, also called 'Young Knives'. The typographic identity and the folk-inspired aesthetic of the artwork reflect the band's origins in rural Ashby-de-la-Zouch. The album cover and booklet document the Whittlesea Straw Bear festival, a pagan custom in which a straw-covered figure leads crowds of people around a small Cambridgeshire town. Images shot on location by Nigel Shafran.

THE YOUNG KNIVES VOICES OF ANIMALS AND MEN

PART TIMER 01 THE DECISION 02 WEEKENDS AND BLEAK DAYS (HOT SUMMER) 03 IN THE PINK 04 MYSTIC ENERGY 05 HERE COMES THE RUMOUR MILL 06 TAILORS 07

HALF TIMER 08 SHES ATTRACTED TO 09 DIALING DARLING 10 ANOTHER HOLLOW LINE 11 COASTGUARD 12 LOUGHBOROUGH SUICIDE 13 TREMBLINGS OF TRAILS 14

℗ 2006 Transgressive Records Ltd.
© 2006 Transgressive Records Ltd.
The copyright in this sound recording and artwork is owned by Transgressive Records Ltd. Unauthorised copying, hiring, lending, public performance and broadcasting prohibited.
All rights reserved. Made in the EU.
TRANS036CD/2564634512.

www.theyoungknives.com
www.transgressiverecords.co.uk

Transgressive

19

Voice

Typefaces speak in different tones of voice. Here's how type can manipulate the way we respond to the word 'murder':

Murder
Courier, a monospace
typeface based on
the typewriter,
tells us we are in
the realm of the
police procedural.

Murder

Agincourt, a bold Old English typeface style, is dripping with Gothic horror and Victorian sensationalism.

Murder

The same word in Zapfino suggests swash-buckling duels at dawn or the administration of a rarefied poison.

Murder

In Helvetica's clone, Arial, the act of killing someone could be an index entry.

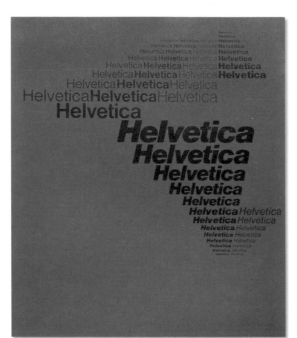

Left and below right: Revered and reviled in equal measure, Helvetica is a sans-serif face with a large x-height. It was designed in 1957 and is now arguably the world's most popular typeface, appearing in applications as diverse as Swiss stamps, airline identities and road signs.

Bottom left: Helvetica has been the official typeface of the Metropolitan Transportation Authority in New York City since 1989. Previous attempts to standardize subway signage in the 1960s used another sans-serif font, Standard Medium.

Each typeface has a particular tone of voice that is capable of enhancing meaning, subverting it or ignoring it altogether. It is a language of its own. What it says – if it says anything at all – depends on who's listening or doing the interpreting.

Nothing illustrates this better than Gary Hustwit's *Helvetica* (2007), a feature-length documentary about a single typeface. Originally called Neue Haas Grotesk, Helvetica was designed in 1957 by Max Miedinger (1910–80) and Eduard Hoffmann (1892–1980) for the Haas type foundry in Switzerland. More than half a century later, it is arguably the world's most popular typeface. It is certainly ubiquitous. A clean-lined sans serif with a large x-height, Helvetica appears on clothes labels, shopfronts, tax forms, posters, traffic signs, packaging, advertising hoardings, computer screens… in fact anywhere and everywhere there are words. Since the 1960s, many international brands have adopted it for their commercial messages. Nowadays, Orange, Gap, Lufthansa and the Royal Bank of Scotland, among many others, are proud to fly its flag.

A typeface that for half a century has been so widely used and in so many different contexts should surely inspire a uniformity of response. Quite the opposite. For some of the typographers and graphic designers who appear in the Hustwit film, Helvetica is *the* classic modern typeface – beautiful, timeless and rational, as functional and reliable as a Swiss clock … pure Alpine air. For others, it is the smog of corporate power and state control – or at best a faceless face, entirely devoid of meaning because the visual world is so saturated with it. If they are capable of arousing such passions, clearly there must be more to typefaces than meets the eye.

The advent of the personal computer, with its inbuilt formatting menu that enables the user to alter the appearance of a text at the click of a mouse, has encouraged typefaces to be seen as a kind of wardrobe for words. Just as you might reach into your closet for a business suit before an important meeting, you can reach into your virtual toolbox and format an email in Times New Roman to signal that your message (and by extension yourself) should be taken seriously. The unanticipated proliferation in recent years of Comic Sans, a typeface with a comic-book appearance, can be seen as another example of this kind of usage. Comic Sans was originally created in 1995 as an appropriate, approachable and readable font for on-screen speech bubbles in software aimed at children. That same colloquial, touchy-feely quality saw Comic Sans become widely adopted soon afterwards for instant messaging. From there it rapidly spread to a disparate range of other applications, including shopfronts, casual notices ('Sorry, we're closed today!') and health leaflets. Given the deluge, perhaps it is no surprise that the detractors of Comic Sans are every bit as vociferous as the ABH ('Anything But Helvetica') lobby, although it seems unlikely that the two groups share much in the way of a common membership.

The expressive quality of type makes it ideal for conveying a consistent personality or image across a wide range of applications, from packaging to advertising. Would you trust a bank that used Comic Sans for its literature? What type of clothing would you expect to find in Gap if it employed a black-letter font for its branding?

Right: Comic Sans was designed by Vincent Connare (1960–) and released by Microsoft in 1995. Originally intended to be used for on-screen speech bubbles, it has since spread to a wide range of other applications. Its detractors argue that Comic Sans is often used inappropriately, in situations where its childish, light-hearted appearance undermines the message or tone of the text.

Overleaf: *Arse*, a print by the British type designer and typographic illustrator Sebastian Lester makes a play of inappropriateness by setting one of his 'favourite words' in a nineteenth-century 'Alphabet of Love'.

In publishing, a typeface can stand as a shorthand for an authorial voice, just as a particular style of jacket tells us to expect more of the same from a bestselling writer.

Simply from the feelings type arouses, it is obvious that much more is going on than the application either of superficial styling or of received notions of legibility. Type expresses the dynamic relationship between content and form, language and sign. It encodes ideas. The interesting questions are where these ideas arise and what they reveal about culture.

Comic Sans

ABCDEFGHIJKLM
NOPQRSTUVWXYZ
abcdefghijklmnopqr
stuvwxyz12345678
90,.:'"/?×<|}{~!@£$%
^&*()±+=

Layout

The relationship between type and the surface on which it is displayed operates both at the smallest scale, in the spaces within and between letterforms, and at the largest, in the context of the whole page or double-page spread.

For a designer such as Massimo Vignelli (1931–), who is rooted in modernism, 'Typography is really white. It's the space between the black.' Postmodernist designers of the 1990s took an entirely different approach to foreground and background, over-running layers of type and using negative spacing.

On the smallest scale, typographers are concerned with the relationship between individual letters, with the aim of ensuring comfortable reading, even spacing and a consistent look on the page. Letters are not equal in breadth however, which means that when certain pairs are combined, the spaces between them will be too wide or too narrow and attract too much attention. 'Kerning' is the process of adjusting letter spacing by working with letter pairs and their counter shapes to create an apparent evenness. In the days of metal type, ligatures that combined two letters into a single linked character were adopted where certain letter pairs (such as 'fi' and 'fl') would otherwise have created an awkward intermediate space.

Right: In the early 1960s the Polish designer Romek Marber (1925–) devised a cover grid for the Penguin Crime series. This proved so successful it was extended to other series on Penguin's list.

Inset: The cover for Dorothy L. Sayers's 1937 novel *Busman's Honeymoon,* was designed using the Marber grid for Penguin Crime.

Below: Examples of ligatures, or linked characters. In the days of metal type, ligatures were used where certain pairs of letters would have created an awkward intermediate space.

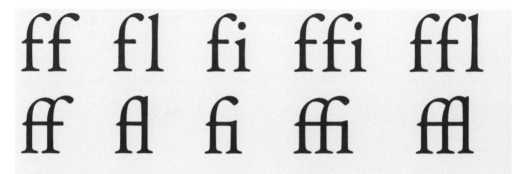

28

Penguin Crime 2'6

abcdefghijk
mnopqrstuvwxy

abcdefghijklmnop

abcdefghjkl

abcdefghijklmnopqr

90°

Penguin Crime 5/-

Busman's honeymoon
Dorothy L. Sayers

Left: This anti-drug poster
issued by the US Public
Health Service adopted
the 'psychedelic' lettering
and graphic style that were
popular with its target
audience.

In a line of text, word spacing, which is fundamentally a function of the font, can be altered depending on whether type is justified or not. Text that is ranged left is often cited as best practice because letter and word spacing will be even. Justified text, which is more conventional, especially in books, results either in hyphenation or in word spacing being stretched or compressed to fill the line.

On a larger scale, the layout of text on a page implies a hierarchy of information, with different type sizes distinguishing between headlines, body copy and captions. Setting a text in two different typefaces – for example combining a sans serif for headings with a serif for body copy – provides an element of contrast that helps to direct the reader's attention.

In magazines, newspapers and illustrated books, it is common for text to be laid out to a grid. In a long text, this provides the designer with a functional framework for organizing material and the reader with a predictable means of orientation. A well-designed grid makes a dynamic use of the relationship between text and white space, so that the white is 'working' as hard as the black.

A grid can also be a kind of signature or brand. The cover grid that the Polish designer Romek Marber (1925–) devised for the Penguin Crime series in the early 1960s updated the image of a well-respected publisher and was eventually extended to other series on its list. The lower two-thirds of the cover space was devoted to an illustration or image, with the top band divided into three for the colophon, series name, price, author and title, all ranged left.

Display typography inevitably places fewer constraints on the typographer and designer. Here type may be said to find its fullest and richest expression. In the work of the American designer Milton Glaser (1929–), for example, type is often treated as an illustration in its own right, arranged into images that create a memorable interplay of sign and meaning.

Process

Typography embodies a tension between the hand and the machine, organic form and geometry, the physical and the abstract. The roots of those tensions go back to the earliest systems of writing, when signs were first adopted to record information and convey meaning.

Every typeface is in some sense a revival of what has gone before, even where the historical narrative is challenged or reinterpreted. The earliest type copied black-letter, or Gothic, handwriting, the standard script of the medieval period. Subsequent typefaces have reflected their own specific medium, from metal type to screen. Even today, when digital processes have seemingly divorced type design from the physical world, the past is still present in letterforms.

Left: *The Book of Kells*, a masterpiece of Western calligraphy, was produced in Ireland c800 by a number of scribes. A transcription in Latin of the four gospels of the New Testament, it was written in iron-gall ink on high-quality vellum. This page, by scribe 'D', shows majuscule script with zoomorphic initials.

Right: Letterforms still bear traces of the tools that were used to produce them. It is thought that the serif originates from the short incised feet that Roman stone-carvers used to finish their letters.

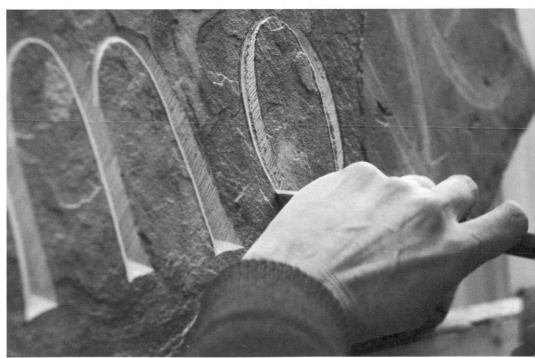

Writing

The earliest scripts, which pre-date the first alphabet, were Egyptian hieroglyphs ('sacred writing'), written in ink on papyrus scrolls or carved into stone, and Mesopotamian cuneiform, made by pressing the blunt end of a reed into a wet clay tablet. Ancient Egyptian, hieroglyphs were essentially pictograms that stood for words or sequences of consonants.

About 2000 BC the first alphabetic script, in which signs or glyphs were used to denote single consonants, was developed in central Egypt, probably so that Egyptian scribes could write down the language of Semitic slave labourers. This spread northwards and became extensively used in Phoenicia, which lay at the hub of a trade network linking west and east. Two key variations of the Phoenician alphabet that subsequently emerged were the Greek alphabet and the Aramaic. The modern Western alphabet is descended from the Greek, while the Aramaic, which became the official script of the Persian empire, is the forerunner of many Near Eastern alphabets.

The pictorial origins of these early scripts are still evident in our alphabet. 'A' comes from a sign representing an ox's head – in Phoenician script what we would call an 'A' appeared on its side. 'T' comes from a sign used to represent a mark, which first appeared in Phoenician as X, while 'O' comes from a sign for an eye.

Writing began with the brush, the reed, the chisel and the pen, and reminders of these tools are also evident in letterforms. The Latin alphabet was composed exclusively of capital letters, or majuscules. Serifs are thought to have originated from the short incised feet with which Roman stone-carvers finished their austere and beautifully proportioned letters. Less formal capitals were used for writing on scrolls, and a cursive script produced by the impression of a stylus on a wax tablet was adopted for more casual types of written communication.

Right: The ninth century saw the development of the minuscule or lower-case letter. Carolingian script, which takes its name from the Emperor Charlemagne, was the standard book hand of Europe for the next 300 years. This example is taken from a ninth-century French manuscript.

cerec illif receffic abeif ec ferebaī incaelū. ec ipfi adoraintef re
greffifunc inbieruſalem cū gaudio magno eceranc femp. inteplo
laudantef ec benedicentef dnm.

INICIVM EVG SECDM IOH

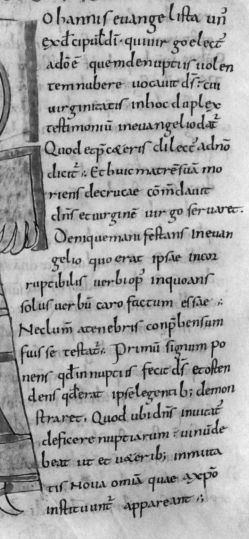

ohannif euangeliſta uñ
ex difcipulif dī. quiuir go electuſ
adeē̄ quemden nupcif uolen
tem nubere uocauit dſ ꞓ cui
uirginitatif inhoc duplex
teſtimoniū ineuangelio datʒ
Quod etpecceriſ dilectʒ adño
dicitʒ. Ec buic matrē fuā mo
rienf decrucae cōmdauit
dñf ec uirginē uir go feruaret.
Deniquemani feſtanf ineuan
gelio quo eract ipſae incor
ruptibiliſ uerbiop inquoanf
foluf uerbū caro factum effae .
Nec lum atenebrif conphenfum
fuiffe reſtatʒ. Primū fignum po
nenſ qd innupcif fecit dſ ecoften
denſ qd erat ipfe legenci bʒ demon
ſtraret. Quod ubi dñr inuitat
deficere nupciarum :uinū de
beat ut ec uaceribʒ inmuta
tif Houa omñ quae axp̄o
inſtituunt appareant :

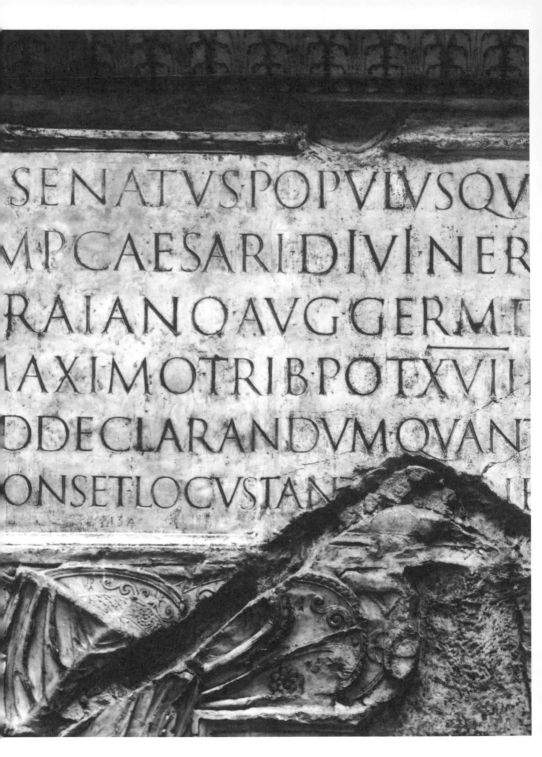

Left and below: The finely
carved letters on the base
of Trajan's Column in Rome
(completed AD 113) are often
held up as models of form
and proportion. Because the
inscription would be read
from below, the lower letters
are slightly smaller than
those above in order to retain
an overall sense of balance.

After the Early Christian world adopted the Latin alphabet as
the book hand for scribes, letterforms gradually changed. As
parchment became more widely available and improved in quality
and size, rounded capitals called uncials appeared, their curves
reflecting a greater ease of writing in ink on a smooth surface.
When books replaced scrolls, there was a shift from writing across
a horizontal surface to writing in vertical columns, typically two per
page to make the most of the available space. The subsequent
emergence of the half-uncial, a compressed majuscule script with
ascending and descending pen strokes, foreshadowed the
development of miniscule letters.

The reign of Charlemagne (768–814) saw the further development
of the miniscule, or lower-case letter, surrounded by its own white
space. Carolingian script was the standard book hand of Europe
right up until the twelfth century, when it was superseded by Gothic,
or black-letter, script.

Throughout the Middle Ages, scribes were confined chiefly to
monastic orders, copying sacred texts and embellishing them with
illuminated letters and illustrations. It was laborious, painstaking
work. Even with the emergence of the first universities, which were
themselves a kind of religious community, books remained rare
and extremely valuable, to the extent that they were often locked
away or chained to lecterns.

By the fifteenth century, the radical movements of the Reformation
and the Renaissance had created a new demand for books.
The logical consequence of the Protestant Reformation, which
challenged the authority of the clergy as interpreters of Christian
scripture, was that lay people would require their own bibles.
The Renaissance, which revived a notion of learning as enquiry,
awakened a thirst for Classical texts and the knowledge they
contained. What printing would soon unleash was the world's
first communications explosion.

The Gutenberg Bible

Printing and papermaking were invented in the Far East more than a thousand years before these technologies became known in the West. When the Arabs introduced papermaking to Europe in the late thirteenth century, Fabriano, a small Italian town near the port of Ancona, rapidly established itself as the most important centre of production. Fabriano craftsmen were responsible for a number of papermaking innovations, including the introduction of the watermark and the use of animal gelatine (rather than starch) to size the sheets, thereby producing a smoother surface. The widespread availability of paper boosted a demand for small woodcut prints, which often included some kind of inscription or motto.

The first book printed with moveable type in the Western world was the Gutenberg Bible of 1455. Each page consisted of two columns of text 42 lines long. The style of the type, what we would call Gothic, or black letter, duplicated the standard book hand employed in written manuscripts, and as such carried an air of authenticity.

Johannes Gutenberg (c 1398–1468) was a German goldsmith based in Mainz. Very little is known about how he came to make his discoveries, but it is clear that his skills and knowledge as a metalworker were of critical importance, particularly in the formulation of the alloy that he used to cast type. He also devised an oil-based ink that was more durable than water-based varieties, and adopted a wooden press for printing that was similar to the olive and wine presses of the day.

The first stage in Gutenberg's process of manufacturing type was to make a master punch from hard metal, with the letter carved back to front in relief at one end. This punch was pressed into a soft metal, such as copper, to make a mould or matrix, which was then placed in a holder. Then individual letters were cast by pouring alloy or 'type-metal' into the mould. The matrix could then be reused. The result was that wherever the letter appeared in the text it always looked the same.

Below: Two folios from the Gutenberg Bible, printed on parchment in the workshop of Johannes Gutenberg in 1455. Each page consisted of two 42-line columns.

Gutenberg's method of manufacturing type may have been a radical new form of mass production, but it was costly, labour-intensive and time-consuming. To print even a single page would have required thousands of pieces of type, which would have taken months, if not years, to make. Even so, the process was to remain virtually unchanged until the advent of the Linotype machine in the late nineteenth century.

The birth of typefaces

If the process of manufacturing type remained the same for many centuries, the *appearance* of type changed almost immediately. Today Gutenberg's Bible appears difficult to decipher because we are not accustomed to the Gothic, or black-letter, hand it was replicating, and we know even less about the contexts in which it would have been read. Scholars or clergy in Gutenberg's day would have had no such problems with legibility. Gutenberg undoubtedly intended his printed Bible to carry the same weight of authority as the handwritten versions it was supplanting.

Given the pre-eminence of black letter as the standard book hand of the day, it is interesting that dissatisfaction with its visual heaviness was expressed almost as soon as printed books began to proliferate. Before very long, new fonts were being created, and by the middle of the sixteenth century printers outside Germany had abandoned the use of black letter altogether, except where its authoritative voice was desirable – in legal documents, for example. In Germany, by contrast, black letter remained a common typeface well into the twentieth century.

What the new medium of printing seemed to be calling for was a new type language. This soon emerged in Renaissance Italy. Here a fine, slanted cursive script was popularly used for written communication. From this script, which was itself based on much older forms, the first roman and italic typefaces were derived. The Frenchman Nicolas Jenson (1420–80) was the first to create letterforms specifically *for* type, rather than translating a book hand *into* type. In Venice, where he had gone to work, Jenson cut the first roman typeface and began printing with it around 1470. His open, round, readable type combined roman capitals with miniscule forms based on the cursive script. The coherent, balanced result created a dynamic use of white space. A little later, Francesco Griffo (1450–1518) cut the first italic typeface, another variant of the humanist minuscule; its compression met a demand for pocket editions of the classics by making more economical use of the page.

Right: Claude Garamond (c1480–1561) based his roman type on that cut by Francesco Griffo in 1495. After Garamond's death, some of his punches went to a foundry in Frankfurt. The 'Egenolff-Berner specimen' showing Garamond roman and italic, issued by the foundry in 1592, is an important reference for the typeface.

Below: A folio from the Aberdeen Bestiary, written and illuminated in England around 1200.

THE BERNER SPECIMEN BROADSIDE OF 1592

41

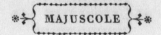

ABCDEFG
HIJKLMNO
PQRSTV

ABCDEFG
HIJKLM

Left: Eighteenth-century roman typefaces were more geometric than anything that had gone before. This example of Bodoni is taken from the *Manuale tipografico del cavalier Giambattista Bodoni* (1818).

Below: John Baskerville was a famous eighteenth-century English typographer. He devised blacker inks and used polished paper to heighten contrast and better display the elegance of his letterforms.

EUNUCHUS

ACTUS V. SCEN

PYTHIAS, CHREMES, SOF

QUID? quid venire in mentem
mihi ?
Quidnam, qui referam facrilego illi g
Qui hunc fuppofuit nobis? *C H.* Mov
Te, nutrix. *S O.* Moveo. *C H.* Video
moves.
P Y. Jamne oftendifti figna nutrici? *C*
P Y. Amabo, quid ait? cognofcitne ? *(*
moriter.
P Y. Bene edepol narras : nam illi fav
Ite intro : jamdudum hera vos exfpec
Virum bonum eccum Parmenonem in
Video. Vide ut otiofus it, fi Di place
Spero me habere, qui hunc meo excruc
Ibo intro, de cognitione ut certum fci;
Poft exibo, atque hunc perterrebo faci

ACTUS V. SCEN

PARMENO, PYTHI

REVISO, quidnam Chærea hic i
Quod fi aftu rem tractavit, Di vo
Quantam et quam veram laudem capic
Nam ut mittam, quod ei amorem diffi

Roman typefaces spread northwards and proved especially popular for printing Latin literature. When these fonts arrived in England in 1520, they were adopted by Wynkyn de Worde (died 1534), whose mentor, William Caxton, was the first English printer. By the mid-sixteenth century the centre of type had shifted to Paris and Lyon, where Claude Garamond (c1480–1561) produced a refined French version of roman type.

Humanist scripts on which the first roman types were based were written with broad-nibbed pens. As these gave way to the pointed pens used in baroque and rococo cursive scripts, the same aesthetic shift was evident in type design. The contrast between thick and thin strokes increased, round letterforms were compressed, and there was greater vertical stress.

Most type used in Britain from the mid-sixteenth century to the mid-seventeenth was from the Netherlands and, much of it was of poor quality. The first major figure in English typography was William Caslon (1692–1766). A specimen sheet published by Caslon in 1734 showed an entire family of typefaces, including roman, italic, Greek, Hebrew and Arabic. His best-known font, Caslon roman, which was widely used in the American colonies, was a precisely cut upright typeface, with a certain old-fashioned irregularity that gave it great charm and appeal. Another renowned eighteenth-century English typographer was John Baskerville (1706–75), a writing master who was much concerned with the aesthetics of letterforms. Baskerville's roman type was especially elegant, and he ensured its optimum presentation by devising blacker, glossier inks and fine polished paper to accentuate contrast.

The first 'true' modern roman typefaces reflected the eighteenth-century classical revival in architecture and art, and were much more geometric than anything that had gone before. Giambattista Bodoni (1740–1813) and Firmin Didot (1764–1836) created typefaces that – with their long ascenders and descenders, fine, precise serifs and rigorous symmetry – expressed the rationalist spirit of the Age of Enlightenment.

WELCOME

A GREAT SPECTRAL AND METEORIC WONDER & NEVER BEFORE SEEN

IGGY FATUSE

WILL MAKE A RADIANT APPEARANCE!

THIS EXPLOSIVE BEAUTY,

— "THE HUMAN FIREFLY" —

Bound By Neither **LAWS OF GRAVITY** nor **PRINCIPLES OF THERMOPHOTONICS**

RIGHT BEFORE YOUR VERY EYES

WILL TRANSFORM

RANDOM ENERGY into VISIBLE LIGHT

TO RENDER HERSELF AT ONCE

WEIGHTLESS and LUMINOUS.

NO ORDINARY ACT OF SPONTANEOUS COMBUSTION!
NO SIMPLE FEAT OF LEVITATIONAL METAMORPHOSIS!
NO MERE TEMPERATURE-GRADIENT INVERSION MIRAGE!

In a Brilliant Aura of Sublime Courage -- WITH NO EXTERNAL SOURCE OF IGNITION -- This Daring Maverick

WILL ELEVATE TO AN EMINENCE

UPWARDS OF

FORTY-FOUR FEET

8X THE HEIGHT OF THIS POSTER!!

before disappearing into a glowing streak in the sky.

44

Left: 'The Human Firefly' (2007) from the *Remarkable* series by Janice Kerbel. The poster was created digitally using typefaces inspired by nineteenth-century letterpress. Silkscreen on campaign poster paper.

Below left: The composing room of the *Washington Post and Times-Herald* newspaper, 1954.

Below right: Student learning to typeset during a printing trades course at Mergenthaler Vocational-Technical High School, 1954.

Overleaf: Individual pieces of movable metal type are sorted into compartments in cases, with the miniscule letters in the lower case boxes and the majuscules or capitals in the upper case.

Industrialization

Although considerable development had taken place in type design in the four centuries since the Gutenberg Bible, the number of typefaces in regular use remained relatively small up until the end of the eighteenth century. All this began to change with the coming of the Industrial Revolution.

Mass production brought with it the need for advertising to distinguish between competing products in the marketplace. Cheap paper became more widely available in larger sizes, which meant public notices and posters could be bigger. To grab attention, letters had to be big, bold and distinctive. Because large letters cast in type metal were heavy and expensive, woodblock printing was used instead, often in combination with metal type. The new letterforms were heavy and bold, with thick 'slab' serifs. Many variations of display type were developed during the course of the nineteenth century, including an emerging sans serif known as 'grotesque'.

The printing process also underwent radical changes. The Stanhope press, the world's first cast-iron press, was introduced in London in 1800 and increased speed and efficiency. In 1814 *The Times* harnessed the power of the age when it became the first newspaper

Left: Twentieth-century poster advertising the services and products of Ottmar Mergenthaler and Co. Ottmar Mergenthaler, a German immigrant to the United States, revolutionized printing when he invented the Linotype machine in the 1880s. The 'hot metal' process, where type was cast in the print shop, hugely increased the speed and accuracy of printing.

to be printed using a press powered by a steam engine. The development of lithography, among many other printing methods over the course of the century, made it easier for illustrations and later photographs to be included in publications. But it was the Linotype machine, introduced in the late 1880s, that was to prove the most revolutionary development. The invention of Ottmar Mergenthaler (1854–99), a German immigrant to the United States, the machine was first used by the *New York Herald Tribune* in 1886.

During the early history of printing, printers both made type and printed with it. Later, the two functions of making type and printing became largely separate, with type foundries supplying type to printers, who would then set it and print it by hand. With the Linotype and Monotype machines, type was cast right in the print shop. The process became known as 'hot metal' to distinguish it from 'cold metal', or pre-cast type. Hot metal hugely increased the speed and accuracy of printing.

Previously, each line of type had to be composed by hand, with the compositor or typesetter picking out letters and punctuation marks from type cases – the upper case on the composing desk holding the majuscules and the lower case holding the minuscules. These were then arranged on a composing stick and then transferred to a wooden tray or galley. It was a slow and painstaking process and prone to inaccuracy.

With the Linotype ('line-o-type') machine, an operator used a keyboard to produce text. The matrices or moulds that corresponded to the relevant letters and punctuation marks were assembled by the machine into a line, which was then cast as a single piece of metal, or 'slug'. The metal used to cast the slug was a mixture of lead, tin and antimony, capable of taking hundreds of thousands of impressions. The Monotype machine operated in a similar fashion, but cast a single piece of type at a time. With the invention of the automatic punch-cutter, which could be used to produce matrices at speed, another type revolution was underway.

49

AN A.B.C. OF GEOFFREY CHAUCER

Incipit carmen secundum ordinem literarum Alphabeti.

AND AL MERCIABLE QUENE,
To whom that al this world fleeth for socour,
To have relees of sinne, sorwe and tene,
Glorious virgine, of alle floures flour,
To thee I flee, confounded in errour!
Help and releve, thou mighty debonaire,
Have mercy on my perilous langour!
Venquisshed me hath my cruel adversaire.

BOUNTEE so fix hath in thyn herte his tente,
That wel I wot thou wolt my socour be,
Thou canst not warne him that, with good entente,
Axeth thyn help. Thyn herte is ay so free,
Thou art largesse of pleyn felicitee,
Haven of refut, of quiete and of reste.
Lo, how that theves seven chasen me!
Help, lady bright, er that my ship to-breste!

COMFORT is noon, but in yow, lady dere,
For lo, my sinne and my confusioun,
Which oughten not in thy presence appere,
Han take on me a grevous accioun
Of verrey right and desperacioun;
And, as by right, they mighten wel sustene
That I were worthy my dampnacioun,
Nere mercy of you, blisful hevene quene.

50

Left: *The Kelmscott Chaucer*, published in 1896 by the Kelmscott Press, featured a black-letter face called Chaucer, designed by the founder of the press, William Morris.

Below: Aubrey Beardsley's work for *The Yellow Book* typifies the late nineteenth-century Aesthetic style, which drew heavily on Japanese influences.

Modernism

Towards the end of the nineteenth century a reaction against industrialization could be seen, first in the Arts and Crafts movement and later in the Aesthetic movement, both of which expressed their particular stances in distinctive typographic forms. William Morris (1834–96) and his followers produced work that harked back to an idealized medievalism. When Morris set up his own press towards the end of his varied career, he designed a black-letter face called Chaucer (1892). The Aesthetes, on the other hand, experimented with stylized letterforms that were heavily influenced by Japanese woodblock prints, as typified by Aubrey Beardsley's work for *The Yellow Book*.

A different sort of reaction was expressed by the radical designers of the German Bauhaus in the early twentieth century. At its birth, modernism was informed by a socialist ideology that echoed Morris's credo of 'art for everyone'. Ornament and decoration were rejected in favour of pure, rigorous form, and the machine, as the engine of mass production, was the inspiration behind the new functional aesthetic. Type became more geometric and pared back. Serifs were abandoned, and sometimes upper-case letters too, as in the Universal typeface designed by Herbert Bayer (1900–85) in 1925. Paul Renner's (1878–1956) Futura (1927) was the first sans-serif face designed for text. Around the same time the term 'graphic design' was coined for the practice of organizing material for reproduction.

Some of the most enduring typefaces from this period were the work of the English sculptor, stone-cutter, typographer and printer Eric Gill (1882–1940). Gill Sans (1926) and Perpetua (1928) have a certain lyrical quality and are based on classical proportions. In 1913 the calligrapher Edward Johnston (1872–1944) was commissioned to design a sans-serif face for London Underground. The typeface is still in use today (as New Johnston), albeit somewhat modified.

In the aftermath of World War II, modernism lost much of its utopian agenda and mutated into an international style, applied across the board to furniture, buildings, products and type. Typography was dominated by the so-called Swiss style, the best examples of which were Helvetica and Univers (both released in 1957). A new type process, photosetting, freed type from its physical base. Previously, letter spacing had been constrained by the physical properties of type – the body of metal on which the type was cast. Univers, designed by Adrian Frutiger (1928–), was the first font to be designed for both hot metal and the new photosetting process.

Paul Renner's Futura (1927), commissioned by the Bauer Type Foundry, was based on the geometric forms of the triangle, circle and square. The first sans-serif face designed for text, Futura was chosen as the typeface for the inscription on the plaque left on the Moon in July 1969.

FUTURA

Left: The distinctive sans-serif typeface designed for London Underground was the work of Edward Johnston and was first adopted in 1916. By the 1930s the typeface had become a key component of London Transport's corporate identity. Redesigned as New Johnston in 1979, it is still in use today.

Right: Sketch by Eric Gill for the 'g' in Gill Sans. Gill Sans, a humanist sans-serif face, was originally created in 1926 and released by the Monotype Corporation in 1928. It won widespread popularity in 1929, when it was chosen by the London and North Eastern Railway (LNER) for use across its entire network, from locomotive nameplates to timetables and posters. Other notable users of Gill Sans include the BBC and Penguin Books, as well as the former British Rail.

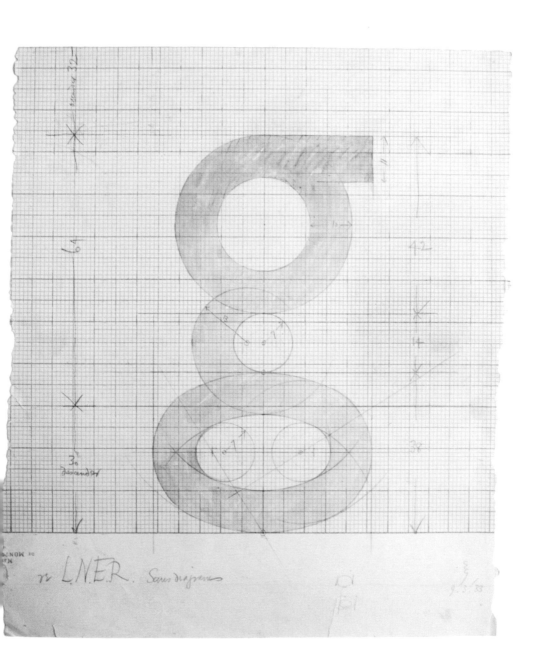

r. L.N.E.R. Sans diagram

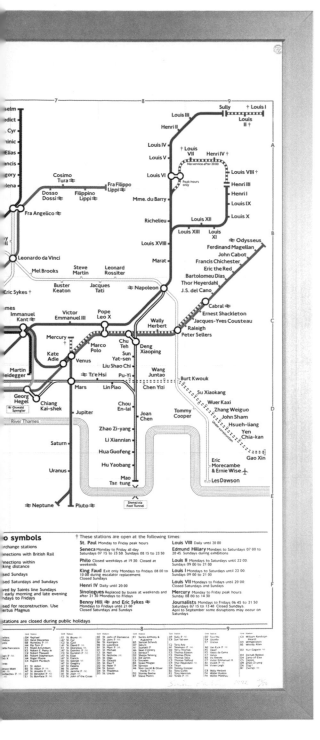

Simon Patterson's playful, subversive lithograph *The Great Bear* (1992) reworks the iconic London Underground map, which also uses the New Johnston typeface. Four-colour lithograph in glass and aluminium frame, edition of 50, 109.2 x 134.6 cm.

The digital revolution

The advent of the personal computer wrote a whole new chapter in the history of typography. The turning point came in 1985 with the launch of the Apple LaserWriter, the first printer to ship with PostScript. PostScript, developed by Adobe Systems, was a new programming language that allowed high-quality graphics and text to be printed on the same page – WYSIWYG, or 'what you see is what you get'. Desktop publishing had arrived.

Left: Poster for 'Fuse' designed by Neville Brody. Fuse is a platform for experimental design and typography that organizes regular conferences and publishes specially commissioned typefaces.

Right: The US magazine *Emigre* (1984–2005), art-directed by the Dutch-born designer Rudy VanderLans (1955–), had a huge influence on experimental typography and graphic design. The independent Emigre digital type foundry, founded by VanderLans and his partner, Zuzana Licko, the same year, continues to develop and release cutting-edge typefaces, including Licko's own. The cover of the nineteenth issue of *Emigre* featured Template Gothic by Barry Deck (1962–).

EMIGRE №19: Starting From Zero

Price: $7.95

Editor/Designer: RUDY VANDERLANS. Editorial consultant: ALICE POLESKY. Distribution, promotion and editorial assistance: ELIZABETH DUNN. Typeface design (this issue): BARRY DECK. Technical support: GERRY VILLAREAL. Emigre is published four times a year by Emigre Graphics.
Copyright ⊚ 1991 Emigre Graphics. All rights reserved. No part of this publication may be reproduced without written permission from the contributors or Emigre Graphics. Emigre magazine is a trademark of Emigre Graphics.
ISSN 1045- 3717.
Send all correspondence to: Emigre, 48 Shattuck Square, №175, Berkeley, CA 94709 - 1140, USA.
Phone (415) 845 9021. Fax (415) 644 0820.
POSTMASTER PLEASE SEND ADDRESS CHANGES TO:
EMIGRE, 48 SHATTUCK SQUARE, №175, BERKELEY, CA 94704 - 1140, USA.
CIRCULATION 6,500. SUBSCRIPTIONS:
$28 (four issues).

(Application to mail at 2nd class postage rates pending at Berkeley, CA.)

INTRRR ODUCT ION

Each time we bring one issue of *Emigre* to the printer, the idea for the next will have slowly started to surface, but never quite crystallizes until we're almost finished.

The idea for this issue started to come together after I was invited to do a three-day workshop at Cranbrook Academy of Art in Bloomfield Hills, Michigan.

I have always been impressed by the graphic design work produced there, mostly because of the students' high level of risk taking and experimentation. Regardless of the methodologies used (some far more interesting than what is expressed in the world, it is their sheer energy and sincere interest in graphic design as a creative discipline that I am attracted to. And although not everything they produce is of the same quality (some work I find downright ugly), the work usually manages to offer something new, raise questions, or make me laugh.

Over the past eight or nine issues, *Emigre* has often featured work by Cranbrook students and alumni alike. *Emigre* №10, published in 1989, was designed, written and produced entirely by the graduate design students.

Just recently a young undergraduate design student from a large university somewhere in the Midwest called me. He had picked up on my leanings towards Cranbrook and asked me whether I thought that any of their 'convention and rule-breaking students at Cranbrook' were ever concerned about contributing to a 'positive' way to use culture instead of always breaking rules. He seemed both mad and frustrated. Mad, I believe, perhaps because he didn't understand this type of work, and frustrated (I found out later) because the school he attended left little room for such personal expression. After suggesting that he should address his questions directly to the Cranbrook students, I did feel a need to inform him that, in my eyes, rule-breaking per se was not the goal. I told him that these graphic designers were trying to find their personal voice and were simply intrigued by the never-ending search for alternative ways to communicate visually and verbally. What better place to do this than in a graduate design program? I also mentioned that he should remember that the conventions and rules that exist within graphic design are not exactly carved in stone and that it is valid to question the necessity of these rules or at least wonder about how and why these rules were established in the first place. Graphic design in not like architecture, where, for example, if you don't follow certain regulations, a building might collapse and kill people.

This doesn't mean that anything goes in graphic design. In the end, it is the designer's goal to communicate messages. But simple common sense is as good a rule to abide by as any.

After my conversation with this student, I decided that this issue of *Emigre* should be devoted to

graphic designers who experiment – designers who are fascinated by the idea of what graphic design would be like if we didn't adhere to the existing rules. It would be so iconoclastic issue. "Why do we experiment?" would be the million dollar question.

However, during my three days at Cranbrook, another interesting notion came into the picture. Whenever the question arose of what the future of graphic design had to store, the students expressed a need to return to simpler, more direct ways of expression. This need had come partially as a reaction to ten years of very intense experimentation with complex typographic and pictorial structuring at Cranbrook (beautifully elaborated upon and illustrated in the recently published book *Cranbrook Design: The New Discourse*). The current students, though, felt a need to take inventory and start with a clean slate. Such a reaction sounded familiar. After scrutiny some of the most unconventional trail-breaking page layouts for the British *The Face* magazine, Neville Brody eventually returned to the very basics of graphic design or, as Keith Robertson writes in the following article, "the safe refuge of the International Style." When visiting Wolfgang Weingart last year, I was amazed when he showed me examples of his most recent work. They were simple typographic designs bearing little resemblance to his earlier layered typographic experiments. Dan Friedman, one of the initiators of American New Wave, is currently entirely satisfied with creating what some might consider non-design. The book *Artificial Nature*, which he designed in 1990, consists primarily of full bleed photographs with short captions set in Futura bold, set as horizontal black rectangles which are each centered in the middle of the page. Even Jan Tschichold, after setting the design world on fire with his manifesto *Die Neue Typographie* (what is considered a safe refuge now was then the most radical approach to graphic design imaginable), would later return to an even safer refuge: classical, center-axis typography. There are numerous other graphic designers I can think of who have traveled this path.

Is this a natural course that designers who experiment inevitably take? Does all experimentation in graphic design lead to the simplification of graphic design? Are graphic designers who concern themselves with complex solutions, merely slow learners who try out the wildest schemes only to come to one conclusion, that less is more? Since we usually raise more questions with *Emigre* than we can answer, this seemed to be a topic right up our alley.

Rudy VanderLans

Left: Barry Deck's Template
Gothic (1990) was inspired
by a sign in a laundromat
where Deck did his laundry.
The sign had been done
with lettering templates. The
typeface that Deck designed
reflected his interest in 'type
that is not perfect'.

The same period saw designers such as Neville Brody (1957–)
defy type orthodoxy. Brody's work for *The Face* turned received
notions of clarity and legibility on their head and prefigured the
grunge anti-aesthetic that later dominated type design in the 1990s.
Type that sampled other typefaces, that was deliberately raw and
badly drawn, or that was inspired by vernacular or 'found' examples,
represented a direct challenge to the conventional idea that type
should be some kind of 'crystal goblet' or clear container for
meaning. Instead, the designer competed with the author for
control of the text, with the reader engaged in an active process of
interpretation. Digital type foundries such as Emigre and Bitstream,
which published much of this experimental work, took advantage of
a growing market for original type design.

At the same time, a number of new fonts were designed specifically
for screen. Screenfonts are either bitmap or outline. Bitmap fonts,
composed of pixels, are designed to be used at a specific size, so
that when letters are scaled up, the digital geometry becomes more
evident. Outline fonts, on the other hand, can be reproduced in high
resolution at any scale, but can be hard to read on screen in small
sizes. Zuzana Licko's (1961–) Lo-Res type family (2001) makes
specific reference to the geometrical basis of screenfonts.

In the early 1990s, Microsoft commissioned the English designer
Matthew Carter (1961–), who originally trained as a punch-cutter,
to design screenfonts for its exclusive use. Georgia (1996), a screen
serif with a traditional appearance, also prints well. Verdana (1996),
a sans-serif face, has since become the gateway to the web. Its
large x-height makes it clear on screen, as does the fact that none
of the characters touch.

The digital age has seen a virtual explosion of typefaces. Within a
few short decades more have been designed than in the entire
previous history of type, aided and abetted by software that allows
anyone who is interested to create their own custom typefaces.
Centuries after Gutenberg's invention, type is now a mass cultural
product with millions of users.

Zuzana Licko's Lo-Res type family was originally created on the newly introduced Apple Macintosh computer using public domain software. Initially viewed as idiosyncratic, more recently such coarse bitmapped fonts have made a comeback for a whole range of cultural and stylistic reasons. Licko also draws on classic sources for her type work. Mrs Eaves, her revival of Baskerville, is among Emigre's most popular and bestselling fonts.

Emperor 8

Oakland 8

Emigre 10

Universal 19

In 1984, Erik Spiekermann (1947–) was commissioned by the Deutsche Bundespost (German federal post office) to design a font for the company, at that time the largest employer in Europe. One requirement was that the font should work well in small sizes on bad paper. These sketches for ampersands show part of the development process for the resulting typeface, PT55. The client decided not to change its existing house typeface (Helvetica), however, and the project was cancelled. Nonetheless, PT55, relaunched as FF Meta, became one of the most popular faces of the 1990s.

Georgia
Georgia italic
Georgia bold
Georgia italic

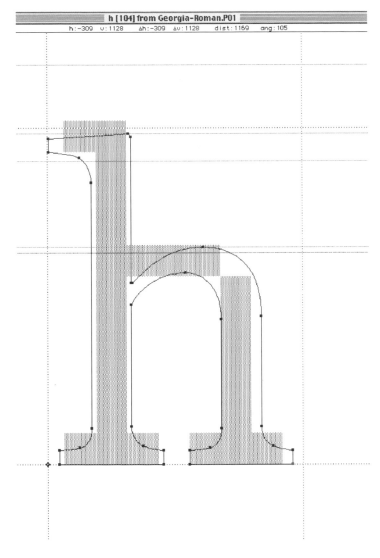

h [104] from Georgia-Roman.P01

h:-309   v:1128   Δh:-309   Δv:1128   dist:1169   ang:105

Georgia (1996) was designed by the celebrated British-born type designer Matthew Carter, who originally trained as a punch-cutter in a Dutch type foundry. Carter subsequently went on to become a founder of Bitstream, one of the first companies to develop type for the screen. By the mid-1990s, as more and more people began spending time on the Internet and using email, Microsoft decided to commission a number of typefaces to be given away with its Windows software. Georgia was one of them. A particular challenge was preventing the serifs from looking too heavy.

Verdana
Verdana italic
Verdana bold
Verdana bold italic

Verdana (1996), the sans-serif font Matthew Carter designed for Microsoft, was one of the defining typefaces of the 1990s and quickly became the predominant screenfont of the web. Carter began by focusing on the characters that are most easily confused – i, j, l and the number 1. He also paid particular attention to spacing. The result was a screenfont of great clarity.

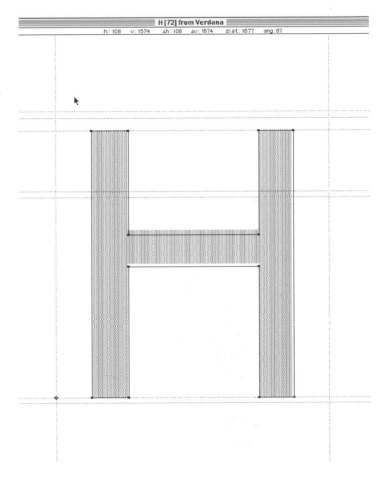

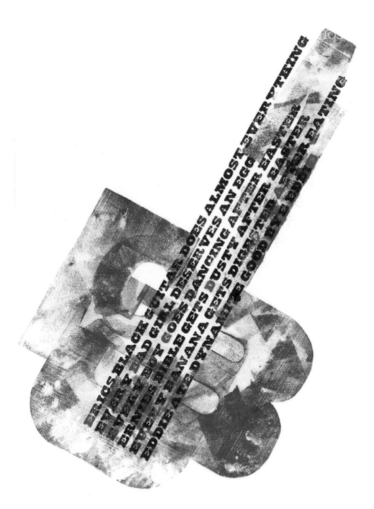

Left: *Homage to Hendrix* (2008), a limited-edition letterpress print by the English typographer Alan Kitching (1940–), featuring overprinted and hand-inked lettering. This print was commissioned by employees at Design Bridge as a leaving present for a guitar-playing colleague. The six lines of copy for remembering the string sequence for the guitar were supplied by the client.

Right: *Rainforest AFLOR* (1999) by Alan Kitching was inspired by the Brazilian rainforest. The wooden letters used to create the print came from a collection that had been stacked on shelves against a damp barn wall. The resulting erosion and boreholes of woodworm beetles can be seen in the texture of the print.

2/17

Spud AF

Aa Bb Cc Dd Ee Ff Gg
Hh Ii Jj Kk Ll Mm Nn
Oo Pp Qq Rr Ss Tt Uu
Vv Ww Xx Yy Zz
1 2 3 4 5 6 7
8 9 0 ¼ ½ ¾
£ € $ ¢ ¥ ¤ @ % ‰ ^ & *
! ¡ ? ¿ / \ / | ‹ › « » ° ` ~
" " ‛ ' ' . : ; , , " " — – _ ® © ™
( ) { } [ ] † - × ÷ = ± #
Àà Áá Ää Ââ Åå Ãã
Èè Éé Ëë Êê Ææ Œœ
Ìì Íí Ïï Îî Çç Ññ ß Ÿÿ Łł
Øø Òò Óó Öö Ôô Õõ
Ùù Úú Üü Ûû Žž Šš Þþ Ðð

copyright Andrew Foster 2009

Left: Spud AF (2009) by the British illustrator and designer Andrew Foster is a font in which all the characters have been created by cutting and printing with potatoes. This grungy sans-serif face makes a virtue of its irregularities and imperfections.

Below: Ecofont, developed by Dutch creative communication agency Spranq, is designed to save ink and toner – between 15 and 20 per cent in comparison with other fonts. The challenge was to see how much of a letter could be removed without affecting readability.

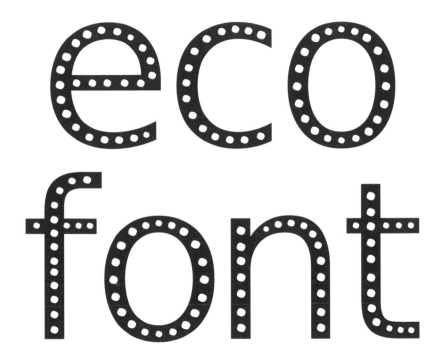

Case study:
Priori typeface

Designer:
Jonathan Barnbrook

Interview with Jonathan Barnbrook and Marcus Leis Allion

Jonathan Barnbrook is one of the best-known creative studios in Britain, specializing in producing innovative books, corporate identities, CD covers, custom fonts, websites and magazines. A multidisciplinary practice combining graphic design, typeface design and motion graphics, the studio works in both commercial and non-commercial spheres. Clients range from the Saatchi Gallery (London) to the anti-corporate collective Adbusters, from Damien Hirst and David Bowie to BBC Radio Scotland and the Mori Arts Center in Tokyo. The studio also produces self-initiated projects, such as original fonts that are released through VirusFonts and used extensively worldwide.

Jonathan Barnbrook (1966–), who founded the studio in 1990, graduated in graphic design from St Martins College of Art and Design in London and took a postgraduate degree at the Royal College of Art. His influential and often controversial work makes strong, provocative statements about corporate culture, politics and consumerism, while his original fonts, notably including Mason (originally released as Manson), Exocet, Bastard and Prozac, display a subversive interplay of language, meaning and letterforms.

Marcus Leis Allion (1971–) has worked alongside Barnbrook since 2001 and played a key role in the creation of many of the fonts released under the VirusFonts label, including Priori. He studied graphic design at the Nene College, Northampton, from where he went on to design album covers for the independent record label Fuel. Today he is art director at LOCA Records and also runs his own type foundry, UNDT.

JB I suppose the first thing we should talk about is the idea behind the typeface. The name comes from '*a priori*', which is a model that people have in their head of an object, so they recognize it when they see it. When you see a shoe, for example, you compare it to a model in your head and you identify it as a shoe. That provided the basis for this typeface, in that it's a series of ideal letterforms where the decorative part of the letterform changes but the basic structure doesn't. So you can have script, sans-serif, serif but they all have the same kind of structure. It means they can interchange. If you use serif and sans serif together in a whole publication, it's supposed to work better. That was the basis of the name.

Did you have specific applications in mind?

JB Priori initially came about when we were asked to enter a competition to design a typeface for Glasgow [City of Architecture and Design] in 1999, but it's an idea I've had for a long time. I've always been interested in doing a font that was very British, and which reflected the environment we're surrounded by here in London. So it referenced things like Eric Gill, lettering on war memorials and street signage.

MLA It was also a development of the ideas that were instigated in Manson. While Priori does take on board some of the ideas associated with book typography, it seeks to challenge some of the ideals of that discipline.

JB It references Eric Gill very strongly. The atmosphere in his typefaces, the idea of Britishness, seems to evoke something that I want to put in my own work as well, although it was much less conscious with him, I think.

Like Gill, you've done stone-carving yourself, haven't you?

JB I did a little bit with David Kindersley [British stone-carver and typographer, 1915–95] and I also did a stone-carving course in Exeter. I couldn't say I was in any way good at it and it wasn't a question of copying a stone-carving hand – we used machines and the machine affected the aesthetic. But I'm very interested in that sort of typography. As a graphic designer what you produce is always very ephemeral, very throwaway. Carving on stone is a completely different way to approach a piece of work because it does last for ever. Serif lettering is thought to come from stone-carving – that's one of the theories. If you're drawing a typeface, it's important to understand the history, I think, because it will help you experiment more. If you understand that things were drawn by a brush or carved, then you don't do the default thing, which is to go to the computer and do a modular typeface.

That relationship with the hand is a sort of tension, isn't it?

JB Letterforms come very much from the way people draw with their hands. Taking it onto the computer has understandably affected the aesthetic of it. But I don't think you can get the understanding of letterforms without doing something manually with them as well. Would you agree, Marcus?

MLA No. I disagree. I think that notions of origin restrict new typographic possibilities by building upon accepted assumptions. It also suggests that there is only one 'true' typography and that everything else is derivative or secondary – which would suggest that the computer, for example, is somehow negated because it comes _after_ the hand. I think it's much more productive to think in terms of technologies and intentions.

Do you draw by hand first?

MLA Sometimes.

JB I do little out-of-focus sketches. I'm not technically very good. The point I was trying to make is that some people immediately go to the computer and they think that's transparent, when it's not. It's one way of working. I wouldn't say I was a traditional type designer in that I sit there and draw everything out technically. It's important that there is a bit of a roughness in the first sketches you do. What the computer is very good at is refining. Because it outputs things in absolute positive and negative, you can see things straightaway, which initially can be quite painful. The computer also allows there to be a process of collage. Although you're not supposed to import other people's fonts, you can reference history or contemporary typography and bring it all together.

MLA I find notions of propriety very interesting. Being able to copy some other design is the foundation of creativity. What Jon would call a postmodern approach to typography can best be exemplified by the emergence of hip hop. While hip hop sampled – or copied – other artists' music, it did so by recoding the contextual signifiers, representing them in new and interesting ways. Digital methods make it much easier to take a similar approach to typography. Jonathan's typeface Prototype [1995] is a great example of such an approach. However, due to misunderstandings over copyright issues and professional self-policing mechanisms, the opportunities to rethink typography are heavily restricted. I think there's scope to open that debate up a lot more.

JB In our book [*The Barnbrook Bible*, 2007] we went through some of the different Priori letterforms and analysed why they look the way they do. For example, 'P' references experiments by [the Bauhaus typographer] Herbert Bayer and the 'A' is from Futura. We wanted to show that typefaces are full of these kinds of references. I think it's important for people to see that you tend to refer to your own landscape when you design.

Aside from Britishness, how would you summarize your landscape?

JB Something that's true to where you come from… but you want to put in things that you're interested in as well, and the relationship with language is important to me. When we draw letterforms we should acknowledge the way language is used to be violent or seductive, or to have no meaning at all.

*From the sketches, then, you'll go more or less straight
onto the computer to refine. What are you refining?*

MLA There are a number of ways to draw characters in order to direct the way in which the shapes are perceived. A perfect-*looking* circle is rarely, if ever, a mathematically perfect circle. For example, if you rotate the 'O' in Paul Renner's Futura by 90 degrees you will begin to see how carefully the character is drawn to account for biases of perception. Therefore, if the designer is concerned with creating an even colour across a typeface, she will need to continually compare the character and space combinations the type produces. This assessment will need to take place at a variety of levels and consider any contextual limitations.

*…Because there are so many components that individual
letterforms share?*

MLA Yes, if you can imagine taking a 'W', which is quite wide and commonly has four strokes, compared to the 'I', which is just a single stroke, what you're trying to do is balance the visual weight between them. In this case, the 'W' will be created using slightly finer 'strokes' that may even taper where they meet or overlap. In this sense, refining means balancing things in order to create an even grey on the page, where no character jars because it appears heavier or out of sync with the typeface's voice.

Where it gets very difficult is with the bolder weights, because you're compromising half the time between achieving enough weight across the font without distorting the design too much. There's lots of little things that you can do, like introducing ink traps, for example.

What's an ink trap?

MLA When Matthew Carter worked with the Bell telephone books, he paid particular attention to the relation between typography and the production process being employed, which in that case was Bell Gothic onto newsprint using a high-speed press. The main problem was caused by the ink spreading, which meant many of the counter-forms in the typeface were filled in, particularly at smaller sizes. Carter's new design [Bell Centennial, 1974] worked with these limitations and incorporated ink traps. When printed, these traps filled with the excess ink, making the resultant character shapes sharper and less likely to clog.

JB One thing you have to remember is that a font is a series of letterforms and not just one. You always have to think about how each one relates to the others. It's a combination both of the aesthetics and the technical side. Because a letterform can be as big as you want or as small as you want, you have to keep trying to find some sort of path through. When you're designing a font like Priori, you have to make sure that when the type's at eight point all the thin parts don't disappear, and that when it's much bigger they don't look really clunky. The first time you do it, you won't do it very well. It's only by comparing the letterforms and comparing the spacing that you will get something.

Priori is your most extensive font, isn't it?

MLA Going back to what Jonathan said earlier, it's extensive in the sense it can never end. There's an alternate set and that set could be opened up again. For example, the upper-case 'A' in the alternate set has the bar dropped down to the bottom, which is a reference to Cyrillic script, something that Jon's been influenced by over the years. However, it's possible to move, scale or replace that one element with others to create another alternate character, which keeps it open. Then there are different styles you could drop onto it. Different clothing for the same basic frame. But that clothing, that style, will also affect the frame, so there's always an interplay between the two.

There were some quite interesting discussions on a few of the type websites when Priori was first released. We have employed it as a 'book typeface' and some people were very dismissive of that because it didn't operate in the way book typefaces traditionally should. And then Priori comes along and begins to disrupt those edges, if you like, a bit. These somewhat conservative guardians of purity would do well to look again at the historical emergence of book typography and the forces that governed it.

JB To go back to basics, the point of drawing typefaces is to get a tone of voice for a piece of text, to say something in a way that's never been said before and in some way to express the spirit of the age. With a typeface you can be expressive in the letterforms, within quite tight restraints. Just changing things slightly will change the tone of voice completely.

That's important when there are so many messages out there.

JB Yes! The conflict between visual expression and the expression of conceptual thoughts is what intrigues me. But it's also about creating something beautiful. Letterforms have the possibility of great beauty. Priori is related to a lot of historical serif forms. I find their authority interesting. And also how people will believe something when it's printed in a certain typeface more than they will believe it in another typeface.

How long does it take?

JB Months! It depends on the typeface. If it's a much simpler display font, it's going to be quicker than doing something like Priori.

MLA Priori took about eighteen months, perhaps a bit longer than that. But there was also other work going on in the studio at the time.

JB It's important not to discourage people. When they're thinking of drawing letterforms, they don't have to do the whole typeface, just a few characters.

Which character do you start with?

JB I start with an idea.

But when you've had the idea, which one do you start with?

JB It depends on the idea.

*Matthew Carter has said that he usually starts with 'h's.
And then moves on to 'o's.*

MLA The 'h' and 'o' are useful as they contain a number of traits – such as width, ascender, stress and so on – that provide a good indication of a typeface's direction. However, we tend to work with words, phrases or ideas that we find interesting and try to express those visually. For example, the notion of *a priori* becomes a way of thinking, and we work with that in combination with other ideas. Interestingly, these ideas may often be unexpressed, but will emerge out of the design process and a certain way of thinking about the world.

Do you know what applications Priori has had?

JB *University Challenge!* You see it on various books. We used it for a few corporate identities. And we used it for the David Bowie's *Heathen* [2002]. We drew some title fonts specially for it based on Priori and used it for the text.

MLA We also used a version of Priori for the design of the Roppongi Hills [a commercial development in Tokyo] identity.

JB Roppongi Hills includes the Mori Arts Center, so we used the serif for the main Roppongi Hills corporate and the sans serif for the subtext. We also tend to use Priori as our main text face in the studio. There was a point when I wasn't using any of my own fonts but that definitely changed with Priori. I think it is a very legible face. And that's something else to point out. If people are drawing fonts, there's no point thinking about what sells and what doesn't. I think you've got to do something that you would use yourself. That's the best way. If not that, then something that you think is an original, an experiment.

If you're going to be creating a voice, it should be your voice?

JB Not necessarily. It can be like writing a song where you take a particular point of view, not necessarily autobiographical. You can be quite extreme. When we release some of the more experimental fonts, we never tend to think so much about whether people are going to buy them. It's just what's right for us, really.

Does it bother you if your fonts are used on products you don't like?

JB It's quite funny, I think. Does it bother you, Marcus?

MLA It used to. Not now, I suppose. In some ways it's quite flattering. But I think initially I had a similar position to Jonathan's in that the conceptual aspect of the designs would be negated and that was very frustrating. Because it was always out of context and there was no way of controlling the context.

JB It's quite funny when people pick up on the most obvious aspect of a typeface. Like the way Mason [1992] or Exocet [1991] has been used as a shorthand for Goth. It's much more complicated drawing a font than that.

You've said people need to bed themselves into the rules before they can break them.

JB Not necessarily. There should always be the possibility to not know anything and do something exciting. It shouldn't be that heavy. The best thing is to just start. I worry that many people are frightened off typeface design because they see it as such a technical, tedious thing. It's about letters, which are expressive.

MLA Again, I think that the term 'typography' tends to be associated with book typography and notions of clarity. All other typography is defined, accessed and judged in relation to this one dominant ideal. I think something can be extremely playful and still be typography.

Also, so many things have been done before. History is not just a resource, but a very good way of understanding and challenging the discipline. It can provide some fantastic insights and is very humbling in that respect.

Aside from Gill, which typefaces do you like?

JB Black-letter fonts are very important for me.

They were some of the inspiration behind Bastard [1990], weren't they?

JB Yes, but I also like them because they are extremely ornate fonts, the opposite of the clear legible things everyone says you should be reading and using. They are so full of character and history.

Quite menacing in some ways…

JB Yes, their association with Nazism is so strong, which is one of the reasons why we called the font Bastard. Previously, when people talked about black-letter fonts, they would completely ignore that association and focus on the history. But I think that's an interesting cultural aspect to those letterforms, not something to be politely ignored. Black-letter fonts were also very popular in Victorian times, when they were used to address the idea of craft in relation to technology. It got to the point where things were so ornate and yet they were being mass-produced and it felt wrong. Some new visual language had to happen because of it. I find the excessiveness, almost campness, of black letter quite amusing. At the end of the postmodernism, when we designed Bastard, it seemed to make sense to really push it and be highly decorative. But it's also about exposing the contradictions.

Johnston is another font that's really important for me. It's very classically based yet very contemporary and just absolutely has the feeling of London in it. If they redid London Underground signage in Helvetica, London would be the poorer for it. I think they've redrawn it and it isn't quite as nice as it used to be.

Also Template Gothic [1990] by Barry Deck. It's a vernacular typeface that he was supposed to have seen in an old laundry and drawn up. It was quite badly drawn, quite rough, but it was from his environment and it seemed to express some spirit of the early 1990s. In terms of contemporary typographers, I think Zuzana Licko is one of the best.

Which typefaces do you hate?

JB When I was younger, I did hate Helvetica. That was the whole reason for me starting to draw fonts, because it felt like it had no character and it completely squashed every other typeface out. It wasn't Helvetica's fault. It was the problem with designers being lazy. For me, the problem was that Helvetica was so heavy with associations. Tutors would say, 'Use this clean, legible typeface,' and you would say, 'No, it's about the 1950s and modernism.' And they would say, 'What are you talking about? It's legible.'

My interest in typography was a complete reaction to that, because I saw that it was about language and history and about creating atmosphere. To me, Helvetica was like unemployment benefit offices. The 'r' of Helvetica really irritates me. I think it's horrible.

Do you think that's because when Helvetica came out at the end of the 1950s it got picked up by corporations?

JB Yes, the ideology of modernism got picked up as well, which was originally quite utopian. When I started drawing typefaces it was 1988: it was quite a rock-and-roll thing to do. It sounds ridiculous, but we were reacting against all that. And it was the first time that people had access to software that allowed them to do it. It was like bands doing their own music and producing it themselves. Some typefaces would last a couple of months and then their popularity would wane. Some would go on a bit longer.

There does seem to be a group of people who think that type should be totally transparent.

JB It never can be, can it? The documentary on Helvetica showed that – people love or hate it and there has to be a reason for that difference of opinion.

When I was younger Trajan's Column was always held up as the textbook example of beautiful typography. What we were asked to do in our type lessons was attain that wonderful proportion. But then again, as soon as someone says something like that, you have to react against it, and there was a definite effort to draw bad type and bring in some element of subversion or reaction.

A lot of the work in the 1990s was hard to read.

MLA But that might have been its purpose – to confuse, confound or question. That's what I think this studio does so well. It always questions those notions, all those assumptions, rather than dismissing them. When Helvetica is credited as being the most legible typeface, we need to ask: who is claiming this? We should also look for other motivations that govern aesthetic decisions.

For example, the Haas type foundry employed Max Miedinger to create a typeface that would *compete* with the new 1950s interpretations of Akzidenz Grotesk [a sans serif originally released in 1896]. Even the name was changed, from 'Neue Haas Grotesk' to 'Helvetica', in order to make it easier to market. Then there was the demand for a visual consistency, which was not instigated by modernism's universal ideal, but by the corporations that began to expand across the world.

JB It depends what you mean by legible. It may not be legible to you. There are plenty of examples where people have done something which is maybe not as legible as you might want, but the message still reaches its audience. There are so many different ways that people read in different types of design.

MLA But this whole notion also suggests that legibility is out there somewhere and that it's attainable as a form in itself, if you can master it, rather than looking at the cultural aspects.

But isn't there a sense that we know what we're talking about when it comes to legibility?

JB I don't think we do. We assume that we do. Get those notions of scientific legibility out of your head! Some people find text completely illegible if it doesn't interest them. If the message isn't open to a particular audience, they won't read it.

Have you always been interested in type?

JB Always, yes. From about the age of 14 or 15. I was interested in drawing the logos of bands in the right typeface because it gave the right voice and connected with their music. So I suppose I must have instinctively understood what a typeface did, even though I didn't know what I was doing. I think a lot of people get into graphics from music. What about you, Marcus?

MLA No, my visual interests were illustration, and furniture and product design. Then I saw Jonathan's design Manson when I was a student and thought that was a very different way of approaching typography, much more of an illustrative approach, which played with tradition.

JB A lot of the typefaces you designed were very aggressive, weren't they? Very political.

MLA Yes, I was very influenced by Jonathan's work. Always the idea first. Then, what does that mean? How do you work with that idea? How problematic can you make things? Rather than resolve a problem, can you create a new one?

Do you think anger is a big part of that?

JB There are positive and negative aspects to creativity. It's a force. All graphic design is contrived to a certain extent. You edit, and you channel visual language.

MLA By presenting certain ideas as being angry or aggressive, it's possible to dismiss work that challenges the dominant ideology. Similar notions have been employed to explain and curtail the actions of others – labelling women as hysterics, for example, or calling people who share music 'thieves'. I think it's much more interesting to pose and pursue questions that destabilize foundations. They represent openings, rather than simple closings.

That questioning is there in the relationship between the font and the names that you choose.

JB Yes, it is, especially when, like Manson, the name was changed [to Mason]. When the name is changed, does it affect how people view the typeface? Naming a typeface is very important, but only for a specific audience. Most people don't know what the names of different fonts are generally, so you are speaking to graphic designers, who if they're intelligent should get what you are trying to talk about.

I think it's interesting how computers change the way you think.

JB Typography should be a reflection of language, absolutely. You do wonder how typography is going to evolve in the next 50 years, because the way people write now is completely different from 10, 15 years ago because of technology. The idea of putting a smiley on a message used to make me cringe, but now I do it because sometimes you have to write a one-line email and you want to make sure people don't think you are being sarcastic. That aspect of communication hasn't really been incorporated into typography yet. The @ symbol, for example, has become a really important character. We always make sure that they're well drawn.

People read differently now, too. They tend to skim the text because they don't have the time. The average time spent on a web page is really short. These are all factors that will influence typography.

Do you use grids in your work?

JB Not at all. Obviously you have a rough grid for a book, a column width and a type size, but that's it. There's no need to design to a grid. There's no point in using them for the sake of using them.

MLA I think they have their place. They're another tool, essentially, but I've never found that tool to be that interesting in terms of what it can produce. Again this studio's way of working is, 'Here's a book. What can we do with a book?'

JB It depends on the project as well. If you are handing work over to other people, then maybe it would make more sense to use a grid, but apart from corporate identities our projects tend to be quite short, so there's no need for it. If you use a grid, it shouldn't be about limiting what you do; it should be about freeing you from having to work out the parameters all the time.

MLA There's a danger of believing that if you just flow the type through the grid it will be correct. Because the grid can come to do the thinking for you, you may not be paying attention to details or question if it is appropriate.

Does it take longer to design without a grid?

MLA No, there are many other methods and approaches to designing a large amount of copy.

How far has your approach been helped by working for yourself?

JB Working for myself was just the easiest way for me to do stuff. It wasn't a brave choice. As long as I survived, that was fine. You can still work for someone else and put forward your view, your philosophy, even in jobs you have no choice about.

But working for yourself must enable you to choose your clients.

JB Yes, but the fonts are not client-based projects. These are personal projects that we release and which are done from an active point of view. I didn't have to start drawing typefaces. It's not like I decided I was going to be a type designer, or someone gave me a job as a type designer. It was a response. I like to see myself as a graphic designer who does type, which will be used by other people hopefully.

What's your approach to working with clients?

JB First we hope that they enjoy working with us. That's the most important thing. We want do something that they're happy with and that we're happy with, either in terms of originality or because we think it's good. There's no point in giving people what they say they want because they might not realize what they want.

Presumably every case is different, but what sort of starting point do you tend to have?

JB You get the parameters of the brief and you try to identify what the problem is to solve. You can either write that down or you can do it instinctively. And then there's usually some sort of discussion in the studio; people are either assigned jobs or we all work on jobs – it's that process of refining again. It sounds corny, but working with a client is a partnership; it's not a war. I think you can do good work and get on with people. It's doesn't have to be confrontational.

To an extent, that is helped if you pick the client or if you are doing something you believe in.

JB You shouldn't work with people you hate. There's no point.

...Or who make things you don't approve of.

JB Same thing. But people know what our politics are, so they tend not to approach us in the first place. They wouldn't be that silly. When we turn down jobs we're not abusive. Either we'll just say 'no' politely or we'll explain why in a clear way. When we turned down a major corporation recently, we sent them a list of reasons why, along with web links, and they phoned up the next morning and asked if the email was a joke.

What did you say to them?

MLA Well, it was a question of pointing out the corporate relationships they endorsed and actively engaged with, and how destructive their business practices were to many disenfranchised and impoverished people. Obviously we're all implicated to some degree in the relationships of capital, but we should seek to challenge that where we can. It's not the sort of thing that comes to the fore in graphic design very often. Even less so in typographic design.

I bet that email got passed round.

MLA I expect it did, but not for the right reasons.

Below: For the competition to design a typeface for Glasgow UK City of Architecture and Design, Barnbrook tried to produce letterforms that were human and appropriate for their context. The idea was to produce a structure of letter shapes on which to 'hang' the styles of the letterforms. The serif and sans-serif typefaces are lower case only, reflecting some of the early twentieth-century experiments to make the alphabet more logical. This is put in a contemporary context, however, with Barnbrook's letterforms being paradoxically 'peculiar' rather than simple. The 'g', for example, is startlingly unconventional.

glasgow 1999 – uk city of architecture & design

sans serif

glasgow 1999 – uk city of architecture & design

serif

glasgow 1999 – uk city of architecture & design

mixing both

Below: In the alternate set of Priori, the uppercase 'A', with its dropped bar, references Cyrillic script.

Right: Ideas for ligatures.

Δ a Β b C c D d E e F f G ɡ H h

I i Į į K k L l m Π n O o Ρ ρ Q q

R r S s T t U u V v W w X x Y y

90

ga gf gg gh gí gí gí
gl gm gn go gr gs gt
gu gy gz ca ky pp qu   of oh oí ol ky pp qu

T AND F THE   H AND E HE

Th TT R TH TE TT   R TH TE TT

EZ FF FI FL LL LA   EZ FF FI FL LL LA

N TH NK NN NT TH   N TH NK NN TE NE

LB LD LE LL LR LP   LB LD LE LL LR LF

ST RS OO OG OC

Below left and right: Priori is a major text face available in serif and sans serif. The idea was to produce a series of typefaces with different styles but with a common core character shape, so they could be mixed together in the same word or text. Reflecting Barnbrook's belief that it is important to be true to your surroundings and cultural experience, Priori borrows heavily from early twentieth-century typography seen in London.

THIS IS PRIORI Serif

In the beginning there was the WORD.
And the Word was VIRUS.

THIS ✦•••••••••••✦•••✦ sans
IS PRI◇RI

In the beginning there was the Word.
And the Word was VIRUS.

Below: Extra character sets for Priori.

Right: One of the applications for Priori has been in Barnbrook's design of the corporate identity for Roppongi Hills, the largest postwar development in Tokyo, comprising residential accommodation, an art gallery, hotel, shops and other facilities. The design of the logo is based on the concept of 'six trees', which is the literal meaning of the *kanji,* or ideograph, for 'Roppongi'. There are six versions of the logo.

Version 1

¶ , . : ;)) ★ ½ ¼ ¾ '' '

Version 2

¶ , . : ;)) ★ ½ ¼ ¾ '' '

Version 1

% ‰ ¡ ¡ ! ? Ä Ë " ï "

Version 2

% ‰ ¡ ¡ ! ? Ä Ë " ï "

Version 1

Ö Ü Ÿ ä ë 'ï' ö ü ÿ

Version 2

Ö Ü Ÿ ä ë 'ï' ö ü ÿ

roppongi hills

roppongi hills

roppongi hills

roppongi hills

roppongi hills

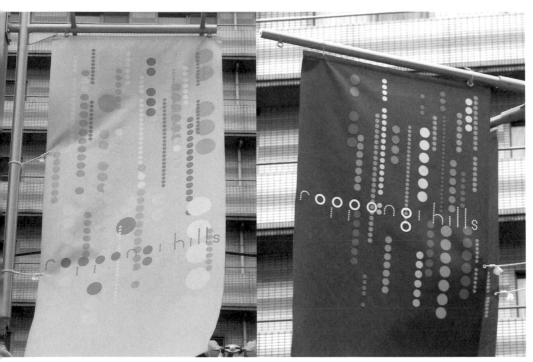

Various applications of
the Roppongi Hills logo,
including environmental
graphics such as murals
and banners.

Another application of Priori was in Barnbrook's design for David Bowie's album *Heathen* (2002). The cover art plays on the anti-religious meaning of the title.

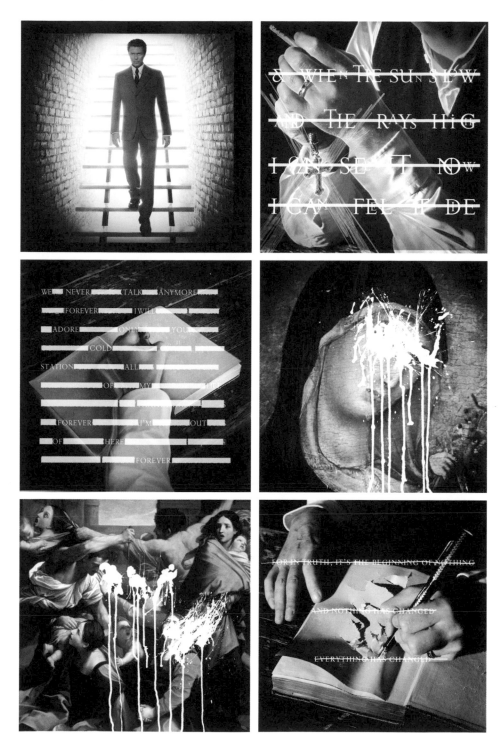

Selected works

Designer:
Jonathan Barnbrook

Bastard, 1990

Black-letter type has been central to the development of typography for over five hundred years. Bastard is a black-letter font drawn with a contemporary eye. Historic forms have been reinterpreted using a set of modular parts and a new aesthetic appropriate to the contemporary technology with which it was produced. In part, the name refers to the font's historical basis – it is a 'bastard' version of a black-letter face – and there was a black-letter font called Bastarda used in the fifteenth or sixteenth century. Another connotation is that where a letterform from the wrong font appeared in a piece of setting it was called 'bastard' type. However, the name was also chosen to highlight and challenge the popular association of black-letter typefaces (used in Germany long after they had died out elsewhere) with Nazism and fascism in general.

Mason has been one of Barnbrook's most widely used and copied typefaces, and companies such as the BBC and Walt Disney employ it to give an ecclesiastical feel to their graphics. Sources of inspiration include nineteenth-century Russian Cyrillic letterforms, Greek architecture and Renaissance bibles. The original font name, Manson, a reference to the notorious serial killer Charles Manson, was chosen to express extremes – love and hate, beauty and ugliness – and to make the face feel contemporary rather than archaic. While 'Manson' sounds elegant, echoing words such as mansion and manse, the association is also with extreme violence and evil. For this reason the name proved controversial, and the font's distributors, Emigre, quickly changed it to the more neutral Mason.

A B C D E F G H I J K L M N   A B C D E F G H I J K L M N

THIS is ⟵

MA[N]SON

O P Q R S T U V W X Y Z   O P Q R S T U V W X Y Z

Mason

PLAIN

A B C D E F G H I J K L
M N O P Q R S T U V W
X Y Z

PLAIN ALTERNATE

A B C D E F G H I J K L
M N O P Q R S T U V W
X Y Z

A SECRET SIGN

TO A

MASON

Prozac was an experiment in making a universal alphabet with as few shapes as possible – the entire typeface uses just six shapes that are flipped or rotated. The name makes reference to the drug Prozac and raises the question whether the letterforms we use affect the meaning of words, or whether simplified letterforms result in simplified communication. The shape of the letterforms also reflects the shape of tablets and capsules.

prozac

a typeface

made up of

six

character shapes

(...)

Drone, 1997

Drone, a typeface that plays around with the idea of poor proportions, comes from letterforms found in the interior of Catholic churches in the Philippines, hand-written texts drawn with a stick or a brush. The letterforms also relate to lettering found in sixteenth- and seventeenth-century England. The name evokes meaningless dogma, or the endless pieces of 'boring' copy set by advertising and design agencies.

THIS IS DRONE

NO 666

FOR TEXT WITHOUT CONTENT

NO 90210

TYPEFACES BASED ON PRIMITIVE
HISPANIC CATHOLIC LETTERING

Olympukes, 2004

Olympukes (Olympics + puke = Olympukes) was born out of Barnbrook's frustration that the pictograms designed for the last few Olympics did not reflect what he saw as the true nature of the event. This series of 'real' pictograms, a self-initiated project released on the occasion of the Athens Olympics, was a witty take on the ultimate design commission, and portrays the complexity, contradictions and skulduggery of the modern games.

DROWNING IN
ADVERTISING

PROFESSIONAL
MILLIONAIRE SPORTS
PERSON TRYING TO
WIN GOLD

UNFAIR
TECHNOLOGICAL
ADVANCE

OLYMPUKES

LIGHT

DARK

107

Index

Glossary

black letter An ornate script, also known as Gothic, widely used in Western Europe in the late medieval period; also used to describe typefaces based on this script.

book hand The formal style of handwriting used in manuscripts before the invention of Western printing in the fifteenth century.

cursive Writing in which the letters are joined up.

Cyrillic The alphabet used by many Slavic peoples, notably the Russians.

font Strictly a set of type in one particular face and size; also used more loosely as a synonym for *typeface*.

Gothic See *black letter*.

grid A framework used by designers to achieve a unified layout in a book or across a series of books.

grotesque Sans-serif typeface developed in the nineteenth century for display type.

hot metal A typesetting technique that uses molten metal to cast type.

humanism The Renaissance revival in learning that looked back to the achievements of ancient Greece and Rome.

italic The sloping form of a typeface, developed from cursive script. Compare *roman*.

kerning In typesetting, the compression or expansion of the space between letters.

ligature In type, a character or letterform comprising two or more letters, e.g. 'æ'.

legibility The quality of type design that enables each character to be clear and easily distinguished from others. This is especially important with characters such as 'i', 'l' and '1', which can easily be confused in running text.

letterform The shape of a letter, numeral or punctuation mark in a typeface; a character.

miniscule Little, or lower-case, letters, often with ascenders (e.g. 'h') or descenders (e.g. 'y').

sans serif A typeface 'without serifs' often used in display faces. In the names of typefaces, it is often indicated by the addition of 'Sans', e.g. Gill Sans, Comic Sans.

modernism The early twentieth-century movement that rejected tradition and sought to establish a pared-back functionalism in art, design and architecture.

point The smallest unit of measurement in typography; in modern computerized typography there are 72 points to an inch.

postmodernism A movement in late twentieth-century design and architecture that rejected the austere strictures of modernism and embraced a new eclecticism and freedom.

roman The 'upright' form of a typeface. Compare *italic*.

screenfont A typeface or font designed specifically for use on screen.

serifs The hooks used to complete the main strokes of a letter.

typeface A design of type, usually including an alphabet, numerals and punctuation marks as well as other symbols.

typesetting The composition of type, e.g. on a page of a book.

typography The art and craft of designing, arranging and composing type.

uncial Rounded, unjoined letters used in early medieval scripts; the origin of modern Western capital letters.

x-height The height of the letter 'x' (as well as other letters) in a particular type size, traditionally measured in points. It is an important characteristic in the appearance of a typeface.

Picture credits

The publisher would like to thank the following photographers and agencies for their kind permission to reproduce the following photographs:

2 Private Collection/The Bridgeman Art Library; 7 Seb Lester; 8 below Bob Rowan/Progressive Image/Corbis; 8 above Bojan Brecelj/Corbis; 9 below Andy Hernandez/Sygma/Corbis; 9 above Andy Rain/epa/Corbis; 10 Matthew Carter; 11 www.nicksherman.com; 12 Ph: Tom Schierlitz/Stefan Sagmeister; 13 Ph: Timothy Greenfield Sanders/Stefan Sagmeister; 14 The Times 3 October 1932/nisyndication.com; 16 below Ted Harris/Just Greece Photo Library/Alamy; 16 above Layne Kennedy/Corbis; 17 JW Alker/Imagebroker/Alamy; 18-19 Design & art direction: Tappin Gofton/Ph: Nigel Shafran; 22 below right Mint Photography/Alamy; 22 below left Diamond Images/Getty Images; 22 above left St Bride Printing Library/Ph: Heloise Acher; 22 above lright Simon Loxley; 23 Rob Wilkinson/Alamy; 26–27 Seb Lester; 29 Taken from Penguin by Design by Phil Baines 2005 ©Penguin Books Ltd; 30 Private Collection/Peter Newark Pictures/The Bridgeman Art Library; 32 ©The Board of Trinity College, Dublin, Ireland/The Bridgeman Art Library; 33 Jacqui Hurst; 35 Bibliotheque Municipale, Boulogne-sur-Mer, France/Lauros/Giraudon/The Bridgeman Art Library; 36 V&A Images/Victoria & Albert Museum; 37 Geoffrey Morgan/Alamy; 39 Universitatsbibliothek, Gottingen, Germany/Bildarchiv Steffens/The Bridgeman Art Library; 40 Folio 101v from The Aberdeen Bestiary/Aberdeen University Library MS24; 41 Private Collection; 42 Museo Bodoniano; 43 The British Library; 44 Janice Kerbel/Courtesy of greengrassi, London; 45 right Al Fenn/Time Life Pictures/Getty Images; 45 left Hank Walker/Time Life Pictures/Getty Images; 46–47 Jacqui Hurst; 48, 50 & 51 Private Collection/The Bridgeman Art Library; 53 St Bride Printing Library/Ph: Heloise Acher; 54 TfL from the London Transport Museum Collection; 55 St Bride Printing Library/Ph: Heloise Acher; 56–57 'The Great Bear' 1992,(lithograph on paper,4-colour lithograph in glass & aluminium frame, edition of 50, 109.2 x 134.6 cm) Ph: Stephen White/Courtesy of Haunch of Venison ©Simon Patterson & Transport for London; 58 Neville Brody; 59–60 & 62 Emigre; 63 Erik Spiekermann; 64–65 Matthew Carter; 66-67 Alan Kitching; 68 Andrew Foster; 69 Ecofont BV, The Netherlands; 71 Des: Barnbrook/Ph: Markus Klinko & Indrani; 89–96 Barnbrook; 97 Mori Building Co. Ltd; 98–99 Des: Barnbrook/Ph: Markus Klinko & Indrani; 101–107 Barnbrook

Every effort has been made to trace the copyright holders. We apologise in advance for any unintentional omissions and would be pleased to insert the appropriate acknowledgement in any subsequent publication.

Credits

First published in 2010
by Conran Octopus Ltd
in association with
The Design Museum

Conran Octopus,
a part of Octopus Publishing
Group, Endeavour House,
189 Shaftesbury Avenue,
London WC2H 8JY
www.octopusbooks.co.uk

A Hachette UK Company
www.hachette.co.uk

Distributed in the United
States and Canada by
Hachette Book Group USA,
237 Park Avenue, New York,
NY 10017 USA

Text copyright ©
Conran Octopus Ltd 2010
Design and layout copyright
© Conran Octopus Ltd 2010

All rights reserved. No part of
this book may be reproduced,
stored in a retrieval system,
or transmitted, in any form or
by any means, electronic,
electrostatic, magnetic tape,
mechanical, photocopying,
recording or otherwise,
without the prior permission
in writing of the Publisher.

British Library Cataloguing-
in-Publication Data.
A catalogue record for
this book is available
from the British Library.

Text written by:
Elizabeth Wilhide

Publisher:
Lorraine Dickey
Consultant Editor:
Deyan Sudjic
Managing Editor:
Sybella Marlow
Editor:
Robert Anderson

Art Director:
Jonathan Christie
Design:
Untitled
Picture Researcher:
Anne-Marie Hoines

Production Manager:
Katherine Hockley

ISBN: 978 1 84091 548 8
Printed in China